CROCHET
Ultimate Book of Pineapples™

General Information

Many of the products used in this pattern book can be purchased from local craft, fabric and variety stores or from the Annie's Attic Needlecraft Catalog. If you need something special, ask your local store to contact the following company.

Yarn:
Wool Worsted Yarn—**LION BRAND YARN COMPANY;** 34 West 15th Street; New York, NY 10011; Phone (212) 243-8995

STIFFENING & BLOCKING
For blocking thread crochet pieces with water, dampen finished piece and arrange and shape on a padded surface. Pin in place with rustproof stainless steel pins; allow to dry completely, then remove pins.

Round Tablecloth

Designed by Dot Drake

FINISHED SIZE:
53" across.

MATERIALS:
- ❑ 3,250 yds. size 10 crochet cotton thread
- ❑ No. 8 steel hook or hook size needed to obtain gauge

GAUGE:
Rnds 1-8 = 3" across.

BASIC STITCHES:
Ch, sl st, sc, hdc, dc, tr.

SPECIAL STITCHES:
For **beginning shell (beg shell),** ch 3, (3 dc, ch 2, 4 dc) in same ch sp or st.

For **shell,** (4 dc, ch 2, 4 dc) in specified ch sp or st.

For **picot,** ch 5, sl st in third ch from hook.

TABLECLOTH

Rnd 1: For **Center Flower**, ch 6, sl st in first ch to form ring, ch 5, *(counts as dc and ch-2)*, dc in ring, *ch 2, dc in ring; repeat from * 3 more times, ch 2, sl st in third ch of beginning ch-5. *(6 ch-2 sps made)*

Rnd 2: Sl st in first ch-2 sp; for **petals**, (sc, hdc, 2 dc, hdc, sc) in each ch sp around, **do not join** at end of rnd. *(6 petals)*

Rnd 3: *Ch 3; working behind petal, sc in next dc of rnd 1; repeat from * around, ch 3, sc in first dc of rnd 1.

Rnd 4: Sl st to first ch-3 sp; for **petals**, (sc, hdc, 3 dc, hdc, sc) in each ch sp around, **do not join** at end of rnd. *(6 petals)*

Rnd 5: *Ch 4; working behind petal, sc in next sc of rnd 3; repeat from * around, ch 4.

Rnd 6: Sl st in first ch-4 sp; for **petals**, (sc, hdc, 5 dc, hdc, sc) in each ch sp around, join with sl st in first sc.

Rnd 7: Ch 1, sl st in any 2 strands at lower back of first dc in petal on rnd 6, **turn** so back of Flower is facing you, *ch 11, skip 4 sts, sc in 2 strands at lower back of next dc on next petal, ch 11, skip next 3 dc**, sc in 2 strands at lower back of next dc; repeat from * around, ending last repeat at **, join at base of beginning ch-11. *(12 ch-11 lps)*

Backs of sts are right side of work.

Rnd 8: Sl st to sixth ch of first ch-11 lp, **beg shell** (see Special Stitches) in same ch, *shell (see Special Stitches) in sixth ch of next ch-11 lp; repeat from * around, join with sl st in top of ch-3.

Rnd 9: Sl st to first ch-2 sp, beg shell in same sp, (ch 1, shell in shell) around, ending with ch 1, join.

Rnd 10: Repeat rnd 9, working ch 2 instead of ch 1 between shells.

Rnd 11: Repeat rnd 9, working ch 3 instead of ch 1 between shells.

Rnd 12: Repeat rnd 9, working ch 5 instead of ch 1 between shells.

Rnd 13: Repeat rnd 9, working ch 7 instead of ch 1 between shells.

Rnd 14: Repeat rnd 9, working ch 8 instead of ch 1 between shells.

Rnd 15: Repeat rnd 9, working ch 9 instead of ch 1 between shells.

Rnd 16: Sl st to first ch-2 sp, beg shell in same sp, *ch 4, dc in fifth ch of next ch-9 lp, ch 4**, shell in shell; repeat from * around, ending last repeat at **, join with sl st in top of ch-3.

Rnd 17: Sl st to first ch-2 sp, beg shell in same sp, *ch 5, skip next ch sp, 4 dc in next dc, ch 5**, shell in shell; repeat from * around, ending last repeat at **, join.

Rnd 18: Sl st to first ch-2 sp, beg shell in same sp, *ch 5, skip next ch sp, 2 dc in each of next 2 dc, ch 3, 2 dc in each of next 2 dc, ch 5**, shell in shell; repeat from * around, ending last repeat at **, join.

Rnd 19: Sl st to first ch-2 sp, beg shell in same sp, *ch 5, skip next ch sp, 9 dc in ch-3 sp, ch 5**, shell in shell; repeat from * around, ending last repeat at **, join.

Rnd 20: Sl st to first ch-2 sp, beg shell in same sp, *ch 5, skip next ch sp, (dc in next dc, ch 1) 8 times, dc in next dc, ch 5**, shell in shell; repeat from * around, ending last repeat at **, join.

Rnd 21: Sl st to first ch-2 sp, beg shell in same sp, *ch 5, (sc in next ch-1 sp, ch 3) 7 times, sc in next ch-1 sp, ch 5**, shell in shell; repeat from * around, ending last repeat at **, join.

Rnd 22: Sl st to first ch-2 sp, (beg shell, ch 2, 4 dc) in same sp, *ch 5, sc in next ch-3 sp, (ch 3, sc in next ch-3 sp) 6 times, ch 5**, (shell, ch 2, 4 dc) in next ch-2 sp; repeat from * around, ending last repeat at **, join.

Rnd 23: Sl st to first ch-2 sp, beg shell in same sp, ch 1, shell in next ch-2 sp, *ch 5, sc in next ch-3 sp, (ch 3, sc in next ch-3 sp) 5 times, ch 5**, shell in next ch-2 sp, ch 1, shell in next ch-2 sp; repeat from * around, ending last repeat at **, join.

Rnd 24: Sl st to first ch-2 sp, beg shell in same sp, *ch 2, dc in next ch-1 sp, ch 2, shell in shell, ch 5, sc in next ch-3 sp, (ch 3, sc in next ch-3 sp) 4 times, ch 5**, shell in shell; repeat from * around, ending last repeat at **, join.

Rnd 25: Sl st to first ch-2 sp, beg shell in same sp, *skip 4 dc of shell, ch 3, 4 dc in next dc, ch 3, shell in shell, ch 5, sc in next ch-3 sp, (ch 3, sc in next ch-3 sp) 3 times, ch 5**, shell in shell; repeat from * around, ending last repeat at **, join.

Rnd 26: Sl st to first ch-2 sp, beg shell in same sp, *ch 4, 2 dc in each of next 2 dc, ch 3, 2 dc in each of next 2 dc, ch 4, shell in shell, ch 5, sc in next ch-3 sp, (ch 3, sc in next ch-3 sp) 2 times, ch 5**, shell in next shell; repeat from * around, ending last repeat at **, join.

Rnd 27: Sl st to first ch-2 sp, beg shell in same sp, *ch 5, skip next ch sp, 11 dc in next ch-3 sp, ch 5, shell in shell, ch 5, sc in next ch-3 sp, ch 3, sc in next ch-3 sp, ch 5**, shell in shell; repeat from * around, ending last repeat at **, join.

Rnd 28: Sl st to first ch-2 sp, beg shell in same sp, *ch 5, skip next ch sp, dc in next dc, (ch 1, dc in next dc) 10 times, ch 5, shell in next shell, ch 5, sc in last ch-3 sp of pineapple, ch 5**, shell in shell; repeat from * around, ending last repeat at **, join.

Rnd 29: Sl st to first ch-2 sp, beg shell in same sp, *ch 5, sc in next ch-1 sp, (ch 3, sc in next ch-1 sp) 9 times, ch 5, (shell in shell) 2 times; repeat from * around, ending last repeat with shell in shell, join.

Rnd 30: Sl st to first ch-2 sp, beg shell in same sp, *ch 5, sc in next ch-3 sp, (ch 3, sc in next ch-3 sp) 8 times, ch 5, shell in shell, ch 1**, shell in shell; repeat from * around, ending last repeat at **, join.

Rnd 31: Sl st to first ch-2 sp, beg shell in same sp, *ch 5, sc in next ch-3 sp, (ch 3, sc in next ch-3 sp) 7 times, ch 5, shell in shell, ch 2, dc in next ch-1 sp, ch 2**, shell in shell; repeat from * around, ending last repeat at **, join.

Rnd 32: Sl st to first ch-2 sp, beg shell in same sp, *ch 5, sc in next ch-3 sp, (ch 3, sc in next ch-3 sp) 6 times, ch 5, shell in shell, ch 3, 4 dc in next dc, ch 3**, shell in shell; repeat from * around, ending last repeat at **, join.

Rnd 33: Sl st to first ch-2 sp, beg shell in same sp, *ch 5, sc in next ch-3 sp, (ch 3, sc in next ch-3 sp) 5 times, ch 5, shell in shell, ch 4, 2 dc in each of next 2 dc, ch 3, 2 dc in each of next 2 dc, ch 4**, shell in shell; repeat from * around, ending last repeat at **, join.

Rnd 34: Sl st to first ch-2 sp, beg shell in same sp, *ch 5, sc in next ch-3 sp, (ch 3, sc in next ch-3 sp) 4 times, ch 5, shell in shell, ch 5, skip next ch sp, 11 dc in next ch-3 sp, ch 5**, shell in shell; repeat from * around, ending last repeat at **, join.

Rnd 35: Sl st to first ch-2 sp, beg shell in same sp, *ch 5, sc in next ch-3 sp, (ch 3, sc in next ch-3 sp) 3 times, ch 5, shell in shell, ch 5, dc in first dc of 11-dc group, (ch 1, dc in next dc) 10 times, ch 5**, shell in shell; repeat from * around, ending last repeat at **, join.

Rnd 36: Sl st to first ch-2 sp, beg shell in same sp, *ch 5, sc in next ch-3 sp, (ch 3, sc in next ch-3 sp) 2 times, ch 5, shell in shell, ch 5, sc in next ch-1 sp, (ch 3, sc in next ch-1 sp) 9 times, ch 5**, shell in shell; repeat from * around, ending last repeat at **, join.

Rnd 37: Sl st to first ch-2 sp, beg shell in same sp, *ch 5, sc in next ch-3 sp, ch 3, sc in next ch-3 sp, ch 5, shell in shell, ch 5, sc in next ch-3 sp, (ch 3, sc in next ch-3 sp) 8 times, ch 5**, shell in shell; repeat from * around, ending last repeat at **, join.

Rnd 38: Sl st to first ch-2 sp, (beg shell, ch 2, 4 dc) in same sp, *ch 5, sc in next ch-3 sp, ch 5, (4 dc, ch 2, 4 dc, ch 2, 4 dc) in next shell, ch 5, sc in next ch-3 sp, (ch 3, sc in next ch-3 sp) 7 times, ch 5**, (4 dc, ch 2, 4 dc, ch 2, 4 dc) in next shell; repeat from * around, ending last repeat at **, join.

Rnd 39: Sl st to first ch-2 sp, beg shell in same sp, *ch 1, shell in next ch-2 sp, ch 5, sc in next sc,

ch 5, shell in next ch-2 sp, ch 1, shell in next ch-2 sp, ch 5, sc in next ch-3 sp, (ch 3, sc in next ch-3 sp) 6 times, ch 5**, shell in next ch-2 sp; repeat from * around, ending last repeat at **, join.

Rnd 40: Sl st to first ch-2 sp, beg shell in same sp, *ch 2, dc in next ch-1 sp, ch 2, (shell in shell) 2 times, ch 2, dc in next ch-1 sp, ch 2, shell in shell, ch 5, sc in next ch-3 sp, (ch 3, sc in next ch-3 sp) 5 times, ch 5**, shell in shell; repeat from * around, ending last repeat at **, join.

Rnd 41: Sl st to first ch-2 sp, beg shell in same sp, *ch 2, skip 3 dc of shell, dc in next dc of shell, ch 2, dc in next dc, ch 2, dc in first dc of next shell, ch 2, 4 dc in ch-2 sp of shell, ch 1, 4 dc in ch-2 sp of next shell, ch 2, skip 3 dc of shell, dc in next dc of shell, ch 2, dc in next dc, ch 2, dc in first dc of next shell, ch 2, shell in same shell, ch 5, sc in next ch-3 sp, (ch 3, sc in next ch-3 sp) 4 times, ch 5**, shell in shell; repeat from * around, ending last repeat at **, join.

Rnd 42: Sl st to first ch-2 sp, beg shell in same sp, *ch 2, skip 3 dc of shell, dc in last dc of shell, (ch 2, dc in next dc) 4 times, ch 2, 4 dc in next ch-1 sp, ch 2, skip 3 dc of 4-dc group, dc in next dc, (ch 2, dc in next dc) 4 times, ch 2, shell in shell, ch 5, sc in next ch-3 sp, (ch 3, sc in next ch-3 sp) 3 times, ch 5**, shell in shell; repeat from * around, ending last repeat at **, join.

Rnd 43: Sl st to first ch-2 sp, beg shell in same sp, *ch 2, skip 3 dc of shell, dc in last dc of shell, (ch 2, dc in next dc) 6 times, ch 2, skip 2 dc of 4-dc group, dc in next dc, (ch 2, dc in next dc) 6 times, ch 2, shell in same shell, ch 5, sc in next ch-3 sp, (ch 3, sc in next ch-3 sp) 2 times, ch 5**, shell in shell; repeat from * around, ending last repeat at **, join.

Rnd 44: Sl st to first ch-2 sp, beg shell in same sp, *ch 2, skip 3 dc of shell, dc in last dc of shell, (ch 2, dc in next dc) 15 times, ch 2, shell in same shell, ch 5, sc in

next ch-3 sp, ch 3, sc in next ch-3 sp, ch 5**, shell in shell; repeat from * around, ending last repeat at **, join.

Rnd 45: Sl st to first ch-2 sp, beg shell in same sp, *ch 2, skip 3 dc of shell, dc in last dc of shell, (ch 2, dc in next dc) 17 times, ch 2, shell in shell, ch 5, sc in next ch-3 sp, ch 5**, shell in shell; repeat from * around, ending last repeat at **, join.

Rnd 46: Sl st to first ch-2 sp, beg shell in same sp, *ch 2, skip 3 dc of shell, dc in last dc of shell, (ch 2, dc in next dc) 19 times, ch 2, shell in shell, ch 5, sc in next sc, ch 5**, shell in shell; repeat from * around, ending last repeat at **, join.

Rnd 47: Sl st to first ch-2 sp, beg shell in same sp, *ch 2, skip 3 dc of shell, dc in last dc of shell, (ch 2, dc in next dc) 21 times, ch 2, (shell in shell) 2 times; repeat from * around, ending with shell in shell, join.

Rnd 48: Sl st to first ch-2 sp, ch 3, 3 dc in same sp, *ch 2, skip 3 dc of shell, dc in last dc of shell, (ch 2, dc in next dc) 23 times, ch 2, 4 dc in ch-2 sp of same shell, ch 1**, 4 dc in ch-2 sp of next shell; repeat from * around, ending last repeat at **, join.

Rnd 49: (Ch 3, 3 dc) in first st, *ch 2, dc in last dc of 4-dc group, (ch 2, dc in next dc) 25 times, ch 2**, 4 dc in next ch-1 sp; repeat from * around, ending last repeat at **, join.

Rnd 50: Ch 5 *(counts as first dc and ch-2)*, *skip 2 dc of 4-dc group, dc in next dc, (ch 2, dc in next dc) 27 times, ch 2; repeat from * around, ending last repeat with (ch 2, dc in next dc) 26 times, ch 2, join with sl st in third ch of beginning ch-5.

Rnd 51: Ch 5, (dc in next dc, ch 2) around, join. *(336 ch-2 sps)*

Rnd 52: Ch 3, 2 dc in each ch-2 sp and dc in each dc around, join. *(1008 dc)*

Rnd 53: Beg shell in first st, *ch 3, skip next 5 dc, sc in next dc, ch 8, skip next 5 dc, sc in next dc, ch 3, skip next 5 dc**, shell in next dc; repeat from * around, ending last repeat at **, join.

Rnd 54: Sl st to first ch-2 sp, beg shell in same sp, *ch 3, shell in ch-8 sp, ch 3**, shell in shell; repeat from * around, ending last repeat at **, join.

Rnds 55-56: Sl st to first ch-2 sp, beg shell in same sp, (ch 3, shell in shell) around, ending last repeat with ch 3, join.

Rnds 57-59: Repeat rnd 55, working a ch 4 instead of ch 3 between shells.

Rnd 60: Sl st to first ch-2 sp, beg shell in same sp, *ch 5, sc in next shell, (ch 5, shell in shell) 3 times; repeat from * around, ending last repeat with (ch 5, shell in shell) 2 times, ch 5, join.

Rnd 61: Sl st to first ch-2 sp, beg shell in same sp, *ch 5, sc in next sc, (ch 5, shell in shell) 3 times; repeat from * around, ending last repeat with (ch 5, shell in shell) 2 times, ch 5, join.

Rnd 62: Sl st to first ch-2 sp, beg shell in same sp, *ch 5, sc in next sc, ch 5, shell in shell, ch 5, 11 dc in ch-2 sp of next shell, ch 5**, shell in shell; repeat from * around, ending last repeat at **, join.

Rnd 63: Sl st to first ch-2 sp, beg shell in same sp, *ch 5, sc in next sc, ch 5, shell in shell, ch 5, dc in first dc of 11-dc group, (ch 1, dc in next dc) 10 times, ch 5**, shell in shell; repeat from * around, ending last repeat at **, join.

Rnd 64: Sl st to first ch-2 sp, beg shell in same sp, *shell in shell, ch 5, sc in next ch-1 sp, (ch 3, sc in next ch-1 sp) 9 times, ch 5**, shell in shell; repeat from * around, ending last repeat at **, join.

Rnd 65: Sl st to first ch-2 sp, beg shell in same sp, *ch 1, shell in shell, ch 5, sc in next ch-3 sp, (ch 3, sc in next ch-3 sp) 8 times, ch 5**, shell in shell; repeat from * around, ending last repeat at **, join.

Rnd 66: Sl st to first ch-2 sp, beg shell in same sp, *ch 2, dc in next ch-1 sp, ch 2, shell in shell, ch 5, sc in next ch-3 sp, (ch 3, sc in next ch-3 sp) 7 times, ch 5**, shell in shell; repeat from * around, end-

ing last repeat at **, join.

Rnd 67: Sl st to first ch-2 sp, beg shell in same sp, *ch 3, skip next ch sp, 4 dc in next dc, ch 3, shell in shell, ch 5, sc in next ch-3 sp, (ch 3, sc in next ch-3 sp) 6 times, ch 5**, shell in shell; repeat from * around, ending last repeat at **, join.

Rnd 68: Sl st to first ch-2 sp, beg shell in same sp, *ch 4, 2 dc in each of next 2 dc, ch 3, 2 dc in each of next 2 dc, ch 4, shell in next shell, ch 5, sc in next ch-3 sp, (ch 3, sc in next ch-3 sp) 5 times, ch 5**, shell in shell; repeat from * around, ending last repeat at **, join.

Rnd 69: Sl st to first ch-2 sp, beg shell in same p, *ch 5, 11 dc in next ch-3 sp, ch 5, shell in shell, ch 5, sc in next ch-3 sp, (ch 3, sc in next ch-3 sp) 4 times, ch 5**, shell in shell; repeat from * around, ending last repeat at **, join.

Rnd 70: Sl st to first ch-2 sp, beg shell in same sp, *ch 5, dc in next dc, (ch 1, dc in next dc) 10 times, ch 5, shell in shell, ch 5, sc in next ch-3 sp, (ch 3, sc in next ch-3 sp) 3 times, ch 5**, shell in shell; repeat from * around, ending last repeat at **, join.

Rnd 71: Sl st to first ch-2 sp, beg shell in same sp, *ch 5, sc in next ch-1 sp, (ch 3, sc in next ch-1 sp) 9 times, ch 5, shell in shell, ch 5, sc in next ch-3 sp, (ch 3, sc in next ch-3 sp) 2 times, ch 5**, shell in shell; repeat from * around, ending last repeat at **, join.

Rnd 72: Sl st to first ch-2 sp, beg shell in same sp, *ch 5, sc in next ch-3 sp, (ch 3, sc in next ch-3 sp) 8 times, ch 5, shell in shell, ch 5, sc in next ch-3 sp, ch 3, sc in next ch-3 sp, ch 5**, shell in shell; repeat from * around, ending last repeat at **, join.

Rnd 73: Sl st to first ch-2 sp, (beg shell, ch 2, 4 dc) in same sp, *ch 5, sc in next ch-3 sp, (ch 3, sc in next ch-3 sp) 7 times, ch 5, (4 dc, ch 2, 4 dc, ch 2, 4 dc) in shell, ch 5, sc in next ch-3 sp, ch 5**, (4 dc, ch 2, 4 dc, ch 2, 4 dc) in shell; repeat from * around, ending last repeat at **, join.

Rnd 74: Sl st across to first ch-2 sp, beg shell in same sp, shell in next ch-2 sp, *ch 5, sc in next ch-3 sp, (ch 3, sc in next ch-3 sp) 6 times, ch 5, (shell in next ch-2 sp) 2 times, ch 5, sc in next sc, ch 5, (shell in next ch-2 sp) 2 times; repeat from * around, join.

Rnd 75: Sl st to first ch-2 sp, beg shell in same sp, *ch 7, shell in shell, ch 5, sc in next ch-3 sp, (ch 3, sc in next ch-3 sp) 5 times, ch 5, shell in shell, ch 7**, (shell in shell) 2 times; repeat from * around, ending last repeat at **, shell in shell, join. Fasten off.

Rnd 76: Skip beg shell on last rnd, join with sl st in ch-2 sp of next shell, beg shell in same sp, *ch 5, sc in next ch-3 sp, (ch 3, sc in next ch-3 sp) 4 times, ch 5, shell in shell, ch 3; for **fan**, work 7 dc in fourth ch of next ch-7 sp, ch 3, 4 dc in next shell, ch 1, 4 dc in next shell, ch 3; for **fan**, work 7 dc in third ch of next ch-5 sp, ch 3**, shell in shell; repeat from * around, ending last repeat at **, join.

Rnd 77: Sl st to first ch-2 sp, beg shell in same sp, *ch 5, sc in next ch-3 sp, (ch 3, sc in next ch-3 sp) 3 times, ch 5, shell in shell, ch 3, skip next ch sp, 2 dc in each of next 7 dc, ch 3, 4 dc in next ch-1 sp, ch 3, 2 dc in each of next 7 dc, ch 3**, shell in shell; repeat from * around, ending last repeat at **, join.

Rnd 78: Sl st to first ch-2 sp, beg shell in same sp, *ch 5, sc in next ch-3 sp, (ch 3, sc in next ch-3 sp) 2 times, ch 5, shell in shell, ch 3, dc in first dc of 14-dc group, (ch 1, dc in next dc) 13 times, ch 1, skip 4-dc group, dc in first dc of next 14-dc group, (ch 1, dc in next dc) 13 times, ch 3**, shell in shell; repeat from * around, ending last repeat at **, join.

Rnd 79: Sl st to first ch-2 sp, beg shell in same sp, *ch 5, sc in next ch-3 sp, ch 3, sc in next ch-3 sp, ch 5, shell in shell, ch 3, skip next ch sp, dc in next dc, (ch 1, dc in next dc) 11 times, skip 2 dc, dc in next ch-1 sp between fans, skip first 2 dc of next shell, dc in next dc, (ch 1, dc in next dc) 11 times, ch 3**, shell in shell; repeat from * around, ending last repeat at **, join.

Rnd 80: Sl st to first ch-2 sp, beg shell in same sp, *ch 5, sc in next ch-3 sp, ch 5, shell in shell, ch 3, skip next ch sp, dc in next dc, (ch 1, dc in next dc) 10 times, skip 3 dc between fans, dc in next dc, (ch 1, dc in next dc) 10 times, ch 3**, shell in shell; repeat from * around, ending last repeat at **, join.

Rnd 81: Sl st to first ch-2 sp, beg shell in same sp, *ch 5, sc in next sc, ch 5, shell in shell, ch 3, skip next ch sp, dc in next dc, (ch 1, dc in next dc) 9 times, skip 2 dc, dc in next dc, (ch 1, dc in next dc) 9 times, ch 3**, shell in shell; repeat from * around, ending last repeat at **, join.

Rnd 82: Sl st to first ch-2 sp, beg shell in same sp, *shell in shell, ch 3, skip next ch sp, dc in next dc, (ch 2, dc in next dc) 8 times, skip 2 dc, dc in next dc, (ch 2, dc in next dc) 8 times, ch 3**, shell in shell; repeat from * around, end-

ing last repeat at **, join.

Rnd 83: Sl st to first ch-2 sp, ch 3, 3 dc in same sp, *ch 1, 4 dc in next shell, ch 3, tr in first dc of fan, (ch 3, tr in next dc) 7 times, ch 3, skip next dc, tr in next dc, (ch 3, tr in next dc) 8 times, ch 3**, 4 dc in shell; repeat from * around, ending last repeat at **, join.

Rnd 84: Sl st to ch-1 sp, ch 3, 3 dc in same sp, *ch 3, sc in next tr, (**picot**—*see Special Stitches*, ch 1, sc in next tr) 16 times, ch 3**, 4 dc in next ch-1 sp; repeat from * around, ending last repeat at **, join. Fasten off. □□

Beaded Top

Designed by Ann Parnell

FINISHED SIZES:
   Lady's bust 30"-32": Finished measurement: 37". Yarn: 13½ oz.
   Lady's bust 34"-36": Finished measurement: 40". Yarn: 16 oz.
   Lady's bust 38"-40": Finished measurement: 43". Yarn: 17½ oz.

MATERIALS:
   ❏ Microspun by Lion Brand or sport yarn—amount Lily White #100 needed for size.
   ❏ 2 packages 4mm beads
   ❏ White sewing thread
   ❏ Sewing and tapestry needles
   ❏ F and G hooks or hook sizes needed to obtain gauge

GAUGE:
   G hook, 6 shells = 5"; 8 shell rows = 3".

BASIC STITCHES:
   Ch, sl st, sc, dc.

SPECIAL STITCHES:
   For **V stitch (V st),** (dc, ch 1, dc) in specified st.

   For **beginning shell (beg shell),** sc around next st, ch 2, V st in next ch sp, fp around next st, skip next fp.

   For **shell,** skip next fp, fp around

next st, V st in next ch sp, fp around next st, skip next fp.

For **corner increase (corner inc),** V st between next fp and dc, fp around next st, V st in next ch sp, fp around next st, V st between last st worked and next fp.

NOTE:
Instructions are for lady's bust 30"-32"; changes for 34"-36" and 38"-40" are in [ ].

SIDE (make 2)
Rnd 1: With G hook, ch 6, sl st in first ch to form ring, ch 1, 8 sc in ring, join with sl st in first sc. *(8 sc made) Front side of rnd 1 is right side of work.*
Rnd 2: (Ch 4, dc) in first st, **V st** *(see Special Stitches)* in each st around, join with sl st in third ch of beginning ch-4. *(8 V sts)*
Rnd 3: Ch 1, (sc, ch 2, sc) in first ch sp, *[ch 1, skip next st, **front post (fp,** *see Stitch Guide)* around next st, V st in next ch sp, fp around next st, ch 1], skip next st, (sc, ch 2, sc) in next ch sp; repeat from * 2 more times; repeat between [ ], join with sl st in first sc.
Rnd 4: Ch 1, 5 sc in first ch-2 sp, ch 1, **shell** *(see Special Stitches)*, ch 1, (5 sc in next ch-2 sp, ch 1, shell, ch 1) around, join.
Rnd 5: (Ch 3, dc) in first st, 2 dc in each of next 4 sts, ch 1, shell, ch 1, (2 dc in each of next 5 sts, ch 1, shell, ch 1) around, join with sl st in top of ch-3.
Note: *Work sc in **back lps** (see Stitch Guide) on rnds 6-10.*
Rnd 6: Ch 1, sc in first 10 sts, ch 1, shell, ch 1, (sc in next 10 sts, ch 1, shell, ch 1) around, join with sl st in first sc.
Rnd 7: Sl st in first st, ch 1, *sc in next 8 sts, ch 1, skip next st, **corner inc** *(see Special Stitches),* ch 1, skip next st; repeat from * around, join.
Rnd 8: Sl st in first st, ch 1, *sc in next 6 sts, ch 1, skip next st, (fp around next st, V st in next ch sp, fp around next st), shell; repeat between ( ), ch 1, skip next st; repeat from * around, join.

Rnd 9: Sl st in first st, ch 1, (sc in next 4 sts, ch 1, skip next st, shell, corner inc, shell, ch 1, skip next st) around, join.
Rnd 10: Sl st in first st, ch 1, *sc in next 2 sts, ch 1, skip next st, (shell, fp around next st, V st in next ch sp, fp around next st) 2 times, shell, ch 1, skip next st; repeat from * around, join.
Rnd 11: Working in **both lps,** ch 1, sc in first st, ch 2, sc in next st, (*shell 2 times, corner inc, shell 2 times*, sc in next st, ch 2, sc in next st) 3 times; repeat between **, join.
Rnd 12: Ch 3, V st in first ch sp, *[fp around next sc, shell 2 times, (fp around next st, V st in next ch sp, fp around next st), shell; repeat between ( ), shell 2 times] fp around next sc, V st in next ch sp; repeat from * 2 more times; repeat between [ ], join with sl st in top of ch-3.
Rnd 13: Beg shell *(see Special Stitches),* (shell across to next center corner shell, corner inc) 4 times, shell across, join with sl st in top of ch-2.
Rnd 14: Beg shell, *shell across to corner inc, (fp around next st, V st in next ch sp, fp around next st) shell; repeat between ( ); repeat from * 3 more times; shell across, join.
Rnds 15-18 [15-20, 15-22]: Repeat rnds 13 and 14 alternately. At end of last rnd, fasten off.
Note: *For **post st (ps),** work **bp** (see Stitch Guide) on wrong side rows, work fp on right side rows.*
Row 19 [21, 23]: For first shoulder, with right side facing you, join with sc in any corner ch sp, ch 2, dc in same sp, ps around next st, skip next ps, shell 4 [5, 6] times, skip next ps, ps around next st, 2 dc in next ch sp leaving remaining sts unworked, turn.
Row 20 [22, 24]: Ch 2, dc in next st, ps around next st, shell across to last 3 sts, skip next st, ps around next st, 2 dc in last st, turn.
Row 21 [23, 25]: Ch 2, dc in next st, ps around next st, shell across to last shell, skip next st,

ps around next st, skip next ch sp and st, dc in next st, skip next st, dc in next st leaving last st unworked, turn.
Rows 22-26 [24-28, 26-30]: Repeat rows 20-21 [22-23, 24-25] alternately, ending with row 20 [22, 24]. At end of last row, fasten off.
Row 19 [21, 23]: For second shoulder, with wrong side facing you, working in unworked sts of rnd 18 [20, 22], joining in right-hand corner across from first shoulder, repeat row 19 [21, 23] of first shoulder.
Rows 20-26 [22-28, 24-30]: Repeat rows 20-26 [22-28, 24-30] of first shoulder.
With right sides held together, sew shoulder seams.

BODY
Rnd 1: With right side of work facing you, join with sl st in ch sp of center bottom shell on last rnd of 1 side, (ch 4, dc) in same sp, fp around next st, skip next ps, shell across to next corner, corner inc; working along side edge, *shell across to worked corner at beginning of shoulder, skip next fp, fp around next st, V st in worked corner ch sp, fp around same ch between first 2 sts of row 19 [21, 23]; working in ends of rows on shoulder, skip first row, (fp around top of next row, V st in next row, fp around top of same row) 2 times, fp around top of last row at seam, B st in seam, fp around top of next row, skip next row, (fp around top of next row, V st in same row, fp around top of next row, skip next row) 2 times, fp around next worked ch sp between first 2 sts of row 19 [21, 23], V st in same ch sp past first dc, fp around next st*, (shell across to next corner, corner inc) 2 times; repeat between **, shell across to last corner, corner inc, shell across, join with sl st in third ch of ch-4. *Joining is at center back*
Rnd 2: (Sl st, ch 4, dc) in first ch sp, fp around next st, skip next fp, *shell across to next corner inc,

(fp around next st, V st in next ch sp, fp around next st), shell; repeat between ( ); repeat from * 3 more times, shell across, join.

Rnd 3: (Sl st, ch 4, dc) in first ch sp, fp around next st, skip next fp, (shell across to next center corner shell, corner inc) 4 times, shell across, join.

Rnd 4: Repeat rnd 2. Fasten off.

Row 5: For **first side,** join with sl st in bottom right-hand corner shell on 1 side, (ch 2, dc) in same sp, fp around next st, skip next fp, shell across to next corner shell, skip next fp, fp around next st, 2 dc in next ch sp leaving remaining sts unworked, turn.

Rows 6-9: Ch 2, dc in next st, ps around next st, shell across to last 3 sts, skip next st, ps around next st, 2 dc in last st, turn. At end of last row, fasten off.

Rows 5-9: For **second side,** repeat rows 5-9 of first side on opposite edge.

SLEEVES
Note: *Working on 1 size, mark 10th [11th, 12th] shell from center top shell on shoulder on both front and back.*

Row 1: With wrong side facing you, join with sl st in marked shell, (ch 2, dc) in same sp, ps around next st, skip next st, shell across to next marked shell, skip next st, ps around next st, 2 dc in next ch sp, turn. *(19 shells made)* [21 shells made, 23 shells made]

Row 2: Ch 2, ps around next st, skip next st, shell across to last 3 sts, skip next st, ps around next st, dc in last st, turn.

Row 3: Ch 2, skip next st, shell across to last 2 sts, skip next st, dc in last st, turn.

Row 4: Ch 2, V st in next shell, ps around next st, shell across to last shell, skip next st, ps around next st, V st in next ch sp, skip next 2 sts, dc in last st, turn. *(17)* [19, 21]

Row 5: Ch 2, skip next st, dc in next ch sp, ps around next st, shell across to last shell, skip next st, ps around next st, dc in next ch sp, skip next st, dc in last st, turn.

Rows 6-9: For **sizes 30-32" and 34"-36"** only, repeat rows 2-5.

Rows 10-18 [10-18, 6-18]: For **all sizes,** ch 2, dc in next st, ps around next st, shell across to last 3 sts, skip next st, ps around next st, 2 dc in last st, turn. At end of last row, fasten off.

Repeat on other side for other Sleeve.

Sew side and Sleeve seams.

NECK EDGING
Rnd 1: With right side facing you, working in sts and ends of rows around neck opening, with F hook, join with sc at seam; spacing sts so edge lays flat, sc around, ending with even number of sts, join with sl st in first sc.

Rnd 2: Ch 1, (sc, ch 3, sc) in first st, skip next st, *(sc, ch 3, sc) in next st, skip next st; repeat from * around, join. Fasten off.

Sew one bead to rnd 1 below every other ch-3 sp.

SLEEVE EDGING
Working on last row of Sleeve, work same as Neck Edging.

Repeat on other Sleeve.

Sew one bead below every other ch-3 sp.

BOTTOM EDGING
Working in sts and in ends of rows around bottom edge, work same as Neck Edging.

Sew one bead to each st of rnd 1 and 19 beads around each pineapple on front.❏❑

Doily

Designed by Erma Fielder

FINISHED SIZE:
12½" diameter.

MATERIALS:
- ❑ 250 yds. size 10 crochet cotton thread
- ❑ No. 7 steel hook or hook size needed to obtain gauge

GAUGE:
10 dc = 1"; 8 dc rows = 2".

BASIC STITCHES:
Ch, sl st, sc, hdc, dc, tr.

SPECIAL STITCH:
For **shell,** (2 dc, ch 2, 2 dc) in specified sp.

NOTE:
Do not work in dc of shells unless otherwise stated.

DOILY

Rnd 1: Ch 12, sl st in first ch to form ring, ch 1, 24 sc in ring, join with sl st in first sc. *(24 sc made)*

Rnd 2: Ch 1, (sc in next 5 sts, sl st in next st, ch 15, sl st in same st) around, join. *(20 sc, 4 ch-15 sps)*

Rnd 3: Ch 1, sc in first 5 sts, 31 sc in next ch-15 sp, (sc in next 5 sts, 31 sc in next ch-15 sp) around, join. *(144 sc)*

Rnd 4: Sl st across first 8 sts, ch 4 *(counts as first dc and ch-1)*, skip next st, dc in next st, (ch 1, skip next st, dc in next st) 12 times, *skip next 9 sts, dc in next st, (ch 1, skip next st, dc in next st) 13 times; repeat from * 2 more times, skip last 2 sts, join with sl st in third ch of beginning ch-4. *(56 dc)*

Rnd 5: Sl st in first ch-1 sp, ch 3 *(counts as first dc)*, *dc in next 5 ch-1 sps, **shell** (see Special Stitch) in next sp, dc in next 6 ch sps, ch 2, skip 2 dc**, dc in next ch-1 sp; repeat from * around, ending last repeat at **, join with sl st in top of ch-3.

Rnd 6: Ch 3, dc in next 5 sts, *ch

2, (shell, ch 2, 2 dc) in shell, ch 2, dc in next 6 sts, shell in ch-2 sp**, dc in next 6 sts; repeat from * around, ending last repeat at **, join.

Rnd 7: Ch 3, dc in next 5 dc, *ch 2, skip next ch-2 sp, shell in shell, ch 2, shell in next ch-2 sp, ch 2, dc in next 6 dc, ch 1, shell in shell, ch 1**, dc in next 6 dc; repeat from * around, ending last repeat at **, join.

Rnd 8: Ch 3, dc in next 5 dc, *ch 2, shell in shell, shell in next ch-2 sp, shell in shell, ch 2, dc in next 6 dc, ch 1, (shell, ch 2, 2 dc) in next shell, ch 1**, dc in next 6 dc; repeat from * around, ending last repeat at **, join.

Rnd 9: Ch 3, dc in next 5 dc, *ch 2, shell in shell, (ch 1, shell in shell) 2 times, ch 2, dc in next 6 dc, ch 1, shell in shell, ch 1, shell in next ch-2 sp, ch 1**, dc in next 6 dc; repeat from * around, ending last repeat at **, join.

Rnd 10: Ch 3, dc in next 5 dc, *ch 2, shell in shell, ch 2, (2 dc, ch 5, 2 dc) in next shell, ch 2, shell in shell, ch 2, dc in next 6 dc, ch 1, shell in shell, dc in ch-1 sp, shell in shell, ch 1**, dc in next 6 dc; repeat from * around, ending last repeat at **, join.

Rnd 11: Ch 3, dc in next 5 dc, *ch 2, shell in shell, ch 3, 13 tr in next ch-5 sp, ch 3, shell in shell, ch 2, dc in next 6 dc, ch 1, shell in shell, 2 dc in next st, shell in shell, ch 1**, dc in next 6 dc; repeat from * around, ending last repeat at **, join.

Rnd 12: Ch 3, dc in next 5 dc, *ch 2, shell in shell, ch 3, tr in next tr, (ch 1, tr in next tr) 12 times, ch 3, shell in shell, ch 2, dc in next 6 dc, ch 1, shell in shell, 2 dc in next dc, dc in next dc, shell in shell, ch 1**, dc in next 6 dc; repeat from * around, ending last repeat at **, join.

Rnd 13: Ch 3, dc in next 5 dc, *ch 2, shell in shell, ch 3, sc in next ch-1 sp, (ch 3, sc in next sp) 11 times, ch 3, shell in shell, ch 2, dc in next 6 dc, ch 1, shell in shell, dc in next dc, 2 dc in next dc, dc in next dc, shell in shell, ch 1**, dc in next 6 dc; repeat from * around, ending last repeat at **, join.

Rnd 14: Ch 3, dc in next 5 dc, *ch 2, shell in shell, ch 3, skip first ch-3 sp, sc in next ch-3 sp, (ch 3, sc in next ch sp) 10 times, ch 3, shell in shell, ch 2, dc in next 6 dc, ch 1, shell in shell, dc in next 2 dc, 2 dc in next dc, dc in next dc, shell in shell, ch 1**, dc in next 6 dc; repeat from * around, ending last repeat at **, join.

Rnd 15: Ch 3, dc in next 5 dc, *ch 2, shell in shell, ch 3, skip first ch-3 sp, sc in next ch-3 sp, (ch 3, sc in next ch sp) 9 times, ch 3, shell in shell, ch 2, dc in next 6 dc, ch 1, shell in shell, dc in next 2 dc, 2 dc in next dc, dc in next 2 dc, shell in shell, ch 1**, dc in next 6 dc; repeat from * around, ending last repeat at **, join.

Rnd 16: Ch 3, dc in next 5 dc, *ch 2, shell in shell, ch 3, skip first ch-3 sp, sc in next ch-3 sp, (ch 3, sc in next ch sp) 8 times, ch 3, shell in shell, ch 2, dc in next 6 dc, ch 1, shell in shell, dc in next 6 dc, shell in shell, ch 1**, dc in next 6 dc; repeat from * around, ending last repeat at **, join.

Rnd 17: Ch 3, dc in next 5 dc, *ch 2, shell in shell, ch 3, skip first ch-3 sp, sc in next ch-3 sp, (ch 3, sc in next ch sp) 7 times, ch 3, shell in shell, ch 2, dc in next 6 dc, ch 1, shell in shell, dc in next 2 dc, dc next 2 sts tog, dc in next 2 dc, shell in shell, ch 1**, dc in next 6 dc; repeat from * around, ending last repeat at **, join.

Rnd 18: Ch 3, dc in next 5 dc, *ch 2, shell in shell, ch 3, skip first ch-3 sp, sc in next ch-3 sp, (ch 3, sc in next ch sp) 6 times, ch 3, shell in shell, ch 2, dc in next 6 dc, ch 1, shell in shell, dc in next st, dc next 2 sts tog, dc in next 2 dc,

shell in shell, ch 1**, dc in next 6 dc; repeat from * around, ending last repeat at **, join.

Rnd 19: Ch 3, dc in next 5 dc, *ch 2, sc in next ch-2 sp, ch 2, shell in shell, ch 3, skip first ch-3 sp, sc in next ch-3 sp, (ch 3, sc in next ch sp) 5 times, ch 3, shell in shell, ch 2, sc in next ch-2 sp, ch 2, dc in next 6 dc, ch 2, sc in next ch-1 sp, ch 2, shell in shell, dc in next st, dc next 2 sts tog, dc in next dc, shell in shell, ch 2, sc in next ch-1 sp, ch 2**, dc in next 6 dc; repeat from * around, ending last repeat at **, join.

Rnd 20: Ch 3, dc in next dc, dc next 2 sts tog, dc in next 2 dc, *(ch 3, sc in next ch-2 sp) 2 times, ch 3, shell in shell, ch 3, skip first ch-3 sp, sc in next ch-3 sp, (ch 3, sc in next ch sp) 4 times, ch 3, shell in shell, (ch 3, sc in next ch-2 sp) 2 times, ch 3, dc in next 2 dc, dc next 2 sts tog, dc in next 2 dc, (ch 3, sc in next ch-2 sp) 2 times, ch 3, shell in shell, dc next 2 sts tog, dc in next dc, shell in shell, (ch 3, sc in next ch-2 sp) 2 times, ch 3**, dc in next 2 dc, dc next 2 sts tog, dc in next 2 dc; repeat from * around, ending last repeat at **, join.

Rnd 21: Ch 3, dc in next dc, dc next 2 sts tog, dc in next dc, *(ch 3, sc in next ch-3 sp) 3 times, ch 3, shell in shell, ch 3, skip next ch-3 sp, sc in next ch-3 sp, (ch 3, sc in next ch sp) 3 times, ch 3, shell in shell, (ch 3, sc in next ch-3 sp) 3 times, ch 3, dc in next 2 dc, dc next 2 sts tog, dc in next dc, (ch 3, sc in next ch-3 sp) 3 times, ch 3, shell in shell, dc next 2 sts tog, shell in shell, (ch 3, sc in next ch-3 sp) 3 times, ch 3**, dc in next 2 dc, dc next 2 sts tog, dc in next dc; repeat from * around, ending last repeat at **, join.

Rnd 22: Ch 3, dc next 2 sts tog,

dc in next dc, *(ch 3, sc in next ch-3 sp) 4 times, ch 3, shell in shell, ch 3, skip first ch-3 sp, sc in next ch-3 sp, (ch 3, sc in next ch sp) 2 times, ch 3, shell in shell, (ch 3, sc in next ch-3 sp) 4 times, ch 3, dc in next dc, dc next 2 sts tog, dc in next dc, (ch 3, sc in next ch sp) 5 times, ch 3, sc in dc between shells, (ch 3, sc in next ch sp) 5 times, ch 3**, dc in next dc, dc next 2 sts tog, dc in next dc; repeat from * around, ending last repeat at **, join.

Rnd 23: Ch 3, dc next 2 sts tog, *(ch 3, sc in next ch-3 sp) 5 times, ch 3, shell in shell, ch 3, skip first ch-3 sp, sc in next ch-3 sp, ch 3, sc in next ch-3 sp, ch 3, shell in shell, (ch 3, sc in next ch-3 sp) 5 times, ch 3, dc in next dc, dc next 2 sts tog, (ch 3, sc in next ch-3 sp) 12 times, ch 3**, dc in next dc, dc next 2 sts tog; repeat from * around, ending last repeat at **, join.

Rnd 24: (Ch 3, sc in next ch-3 sp) 6 times, ch 3, *shell in shell, ch 3, skip next ch-3 sp, sc in next ch-3 sp, ch 3, shell in shell, (ch 3, sc in next ch-3 sp) 25 times, ch 3; repeat from * around, ending last repeat with (ch 3, sc in next ch-3 sp) 18 times, ch 3, join with sl st in base of beginning ch-3.

Rnd 25: Sl st to second ch of first ch-3, (ch 3, sc in next ch-3 sp) 6 times, ch 3, *(shell in shell) 2 times, (ch 3, sc in next ch-3 sp) 26 times, ch 3; repeat from * around, ending last repeat with (ch 3, sc in next ch-3 sp) 19 times, ch 3, join with sl st in base of beginning ch-3.

Rnd 26: Sl st to second ch of next ch-3, (ch 3, sc in next ch sp) around, ending with ch 3, join with sl st in base of ch-3.

Rnd 27: Ch 1, (sc, hdc, dc, hdc, sc) in each ch sp around, join with sl st in first sc. Fasten off.❏❏

Hot Pad

Designed by Marie Jones

FINISHED SIZE:
8" long

MATERIALS:
- 1¾ oz. cotton worsted yarn
- H hook or hook size needed to obtain gauge

GAUGE:
4 sc = 1"; 4 sc rows = 1"; 1 tr row = 1"; 3 shell rows = 2".

BASIC STITCHES:
Ch, sl st, sc, dc, tr.

SPECIAL STITCH:
For **shell,** (2 dc, ch 2, 2 dc) in specified st.

HOT PAD
Row 1: With 2 strands held together, ch 4, (2 dc, ch 2, 3 dc) in fourth ch from hook, turn. *(6 dc made)*
Row 2: Ch 4, skip next 2 sts, (3 dc, ch 2, 3 dc, ch 2, 3 dc) in next ch sp leaving last 3 sts unworked, turn. *(9 dc)*
Row 3: Ch 4, skip next 2 sts, **shell** *(see Special Stitch)* in first ch-2 sp,

ch 3, skip next 3 sts, (dc, ch 4, dc) in next ch-2 sp, skip next 3 sts, shell in last ch-4 sp, turn. *(2 shells, 2 dc)*
Row 4: Ch 4, shell in ch sp of first shell, ch 3, skip next ch-3 sp and next dc, 15 tr in next ch-4 sp, ch 3, skip next ch-3 sp, shell in ch sp of last shell, turn. *(2 shells, 15 tr)*
Row 5: Ch 4, shell in first shell, ch 3, skip next ch sp, sc in next 15 sts, ch 3, skip next ch sp, shell in last shell, turn.
Rows 6-7: Ch 4, shell in first shell, ch 3, skip next ch sp and next sc, sc in each sc across to last sc, ch 3, skip next sc and next ch sp, shell in last shell, turn. At end of last row *(2 shells, 11 sc).*
Rows 8-10: Ch 4, shell in first shell, ch 4, skip next ch sp and next sc, sc in each sc across to last sc, ch 4, skip next sc and next ch sp, shell in last shell, turn. At end of last row *(2 shells, 5 sc).*
Row 11: Ch 4, shell in first shell, ch 5, skip next ch sp and next sc, sc in next 3 sc, ch 5, skip next sc and next ch sp, shell in last shell, turn. *(2 shells, 3 sc)*
Row 12: Ch 4, shell in first shell, ch 6, skip next ch sp and next sc, sc in next sc, ch 6, skip next sc and next ch sp, shell in last shell, turn. *(2 shells, 1 sc)*
Row 13: Ch 4, shell in first shell, skip next 2 ch sps and sc, shell in last shell, turn. *(2 shells)*
Row 14: Ch 4, 3 dc in first shell, 3 dc in last shell. Fasten off.❑❑

Butterfly Bow

Designed by Marie Jones

FINISHED SIZE:
7" across large wings.

MATERIALS:
- ❏ 110 yds. size 10 crochet cotton thread
- ❏ 13 white 5mm pearl beads
- ❏ Hair Barrette
- ❏ Tapestry needle
- ❏ Fabric stiffener
- ❏ H hook or hook size needed to obtain gauge

GAUGE:
3 sc = 1"; 1 tr row = ½"; 3 shell rows = 1".

BASIC STITCHES:
Ch, sl st, sc, dc, tr.

SPECIAL STITCH:
For **shell**, (3 dc, ch 2, 3 dc) in specified ch sp.

LARGE WING (make 2)
Row 1: Ch 4, (2 dc, ch 2, 3 dc) in fourth ch from hook, turn. *(6 dc made)*

Row 2: Ch 4, skip next 2 sts, (3 dc, ch 2, 3 dc, ch 2, 3 dc) in ch sp, turn. *(9 dc)*

Row 3: Ch 4, skip next 2 sts, **shell** *(see Special Stitch)* in first ch sp, ch 4, shell in next ch sp, turn. *(2 shells)*

Row 4: Ch 4, shell in ch sp of first shell, ch 3, (dc, ch 4, dc) in next ch sp, ch 3, shell in ch sp of last shell, turn.

Row 5: Ch 4, shell in first shell, ch 4, skip next ch sp, 15 tr in next ch sp, ch 4, skip next ch sp, shell in last shell, turn. *(2 shells, 15 tr)*

Row 6: Ch 4, shell in first shell, ch 4, skip next ch sp, sc in each tr across, ch 4, skip next ch sp, shell in last shell, turn.

Rows 7-12: Ch 4, shell in first shell, ch 5, skip next ch sp and next sc, sc in each sc across to last sc, ch 5, skip last sc and next ch sp, shell in last shell, turn. At end of last row *(2 shells, 3 sc).*

Row 13: Ch 4, shell in first shell, ch 6, skip next ch sp and next sc, sc in next sc, ch 6, skip next sc and next ch sp, shell in last shell, turn.

Row 14: Ch 4, shell in first shell, skip next 2 ch sps and sc, shell in last shell, turn. *(2 shells)* For **first Wing,** fasten off; for **second Wing,** do not fasten off.

For **joining,** sl st in first 3 sts on second Wing; hold first and second Wings wrong sides together; working through both thicknesses, sl st in ch sp on first shell, sl st in ch sp on last shell. Fasten off.

SMALL WING (make 2)
Rows 1-4: Repeat rows 1-4 of Large Wing.

Row 5: Ch 4, shell in first shell, ch 4, skip next ch sp, 11 tr in next ch sp, ch 4, skip next ch sp, shell in last shell, turn. *(2 shells, 11 tr)*

Rows 6-10: Repeat rows 6-10 of Large Wing. At end of last row *(2 shells, 3 sc).*

Rows 11-12: Repeat rows 13-14 of Large Wing. At end of last row, for **each Wing,** fasten off.

For **joining,** sew one end of row 2 on each Small Wing together. Sew rows 4-6 of one Small Wing to rows 11-13 of Large Wing. Repeat for other side.

BAND
Thread 13 beads onto crochet cotton, push back along thread as you work until needed.

Row 1: Ch 4, 2 dc in fourth ch from hook, pull up bead, ch 3, 3 dc in same ch, turn. *(6 dc made)*

Rows 2-13: Ch 3, 3 dc in ch-3 sp, pull up bead, ch 3, 3 dc in same ch sp, turn.

Row 14: Ch 3, (3 dc, ch 3, 3 dc) in ch sp. **Do not fasten off.**

Wrap around center of Wings, sl st in first 3 sts, sl st center of first and last rows tog. Fasten off.

Starch and block as desired.

Sew or glue to barrette.❏❏

Swan Towels

Designed by Valmay Flint

FINISHED SIZES:
Large Swan is 6" x 6". Small Swan is 3" x 3".

MATERIALS:
- ❏ 450 yds. size 30 crochet cotton thread
- ❏ Hand towel and washcloth
- ❏ Sewing thread and needle
- ❏ No. 10 steel hook or hook size needed to obtain gauge

GAUGE:
6 tr = ½"; 4 tr rows = 1".

BASIC STITCHES:
Ch, sl st, sc, dc, tr.

TOWEL
Large Swan
Row 1: For **body,** ch 6, sl st in first ch to form ring, ch 4, tr in ring, (ch 2, 2 tr in ring) 3 times, turn. *(8 tr, 3 ch sps made)*

Row 2: Ch 4, skip next st; for **shell, (2 tr, ch 2, 2 tr)** in first ch sp; ch 4, shell in next ch sp, 5 tr in last ch sp, turn. *(2 shells, 5 tr)*
Row 3: (Ch 4, tr) in first st, tr in next 4 sts, shell in ch sp of next shell, ch 1, 9 tr in next ch-4 sp, ch 1, shell in ch sp of last shell, turn.
Row 4: Ch 4, shell in first shell, ch 3, dc in next 9 sts, ch 3, shell in next shell, tr in next 5 sts, 2 tr in last st, turn.
Row 5: (Ch 4, tr) in first st, tr in next 6 sts, shell in next shell, ch 5, dc in next 9 sts, ch 5, shell in last shell, turn.
Row 6: Ch 4, shell in first shell, ch 7, dc in next 9 sts, ch 7, shell in next shell, tr in 7 sts, 2 tr in last st, turn.
Row 7: Ch 4, tr in next 8 sts, shell in next shell, ch 7, dc in next 9 sts, ch 7, shell in last shell, turn.
Row 8: Ch 4, (shell, ch 2, 2 tr) in first shell, ch 9, skip next st, dc in next 7 sts, ch 9, shell in next shell, tr in last 9 sts, turn.
Row 9: Ch 4, tr in next 8 sts, (shell, ch 2, 2 tr) in next shell, ch 11, skip next st, dc in next 5 sts, ch 11, shell in next ch-2 sp, shell in last shell, turn.
Row 10: Ch 4, shell in first shell, ch 4, shell in next shell, ch 11, skip next st, dc in next 3 sts, ch 11, shell in next ch-1 sp, shell in last shell leaving 9 sts unworked, turn.
Row 11: Ch 4, shell in first shell, ch 4, shell in next shell, ch 9, skip next st, dc in next st, ch 9, shell in next shell, ch 3, 7 dc in next ch-4 sp, shell in last shell turn.
Row 12: Ch 4, shell in first shell, ch 5, dc in next 7 sts, ch 5, shell in next shell, ch 6, sc in next st, ch 6, shell in next shell, ch 3, 5 dc in next ch-4 sp, ch 3, shell in last shell, turn.
Row 13: Ch 4, shell in first shell, ch 4, dc in next 5 sts, ch 4, shell in next shell, ch 5, skip next sc, shell in next shell, ch 5, dc in next 7 sts, ch 5, shell in last shell, turn.
Row 14: Ch 4, shell in first shell, ch 5, dc in next 7 sts, ch 5, shell in next shell, ch 2, shell in next shell, ch 5, dc in next 5 sts, ch 5, shell in last shell, turn.
Row 15: Ch 4, shell in first shell, ch 6, skip next st, dc in next 3 sts, ch 6, shell in next shell, ch 1, shell in next shell, ch 6, skip next st, dc in next 5 sts, ch 6, shell in last shell, turn.
Row 16: Ch 4, shell in first shell, ch 7, skip next st, dc in next 3 sts, ch 7, shell in each of next 2 shells, mark last shell, ch 7, skip next st, dc in next st, ch 7, shell in last shell, turn.
Row 17: For **wing,** ch 4, shell in first shell, ch 5, sc in next st, ch 5, shell in next shell leaving remaining sts unworked, turn.
Row 18: Ch 4, shell in first shell, ch 3, skip next sc, shell in last shell, turn.

Row 19: Ch 4, shell in each shell across, **do not turn.** Fasten off.

Row 20: For **tail,** join with sl st in marked shell on row 16; ch 4, (tr, ch 2, 2 tr) in same shell, shell in next shell, ch 4, skip next st, dc in next st, ch 4, shell in last shell, turn.

Row 21: Ch 4, shell in first shell, ch 3, sc in next st, ch 3, shell in next shell, ch 1, shell in last shell, turn.

Row 22: Ch 4, shell in first shell, ch 4, shell in next shell, ch 3, skip next sc, shell in last shell, turn.

Row 23: Ch 4, shell in first shell, ch 1, shell in next shell, ch 3, shell in last shell, turn.

Row 24: Ch 4, shell in first shell, ch 1, shell in next shell leaving last shell unworked, turn.

Row 25: Ch 4, shell in each shell across, turn.

Row 26: Ch 4, 2 tr in each of next 2 shells, ch 4, sl st in top of ch-4 on last row. Fasten off.

Row 27: For **neck,** join with sl st in top of ch-4 on row 9, ch 4, tr in same st, tr in next 3 sts, dc in next 4 sts, 2 sc in last st, turn. *(11 sts)*

Row 28: Ch 1, sc first 2 sts tog, sc in next st, dc in next 3 sts, tr in next 3 sts, tr last 2 sts tog, turn. *(9)*

Rows 29-31: Ch 4, tr in each st across, turn.

Row 32: Ch 4, tr in next 3 sts, dc in each of next 3 sts, sc in last 2 sts, turn.

Rows 33-36: Repeat rows 29-32.

Row 37: Ch 1, sc in first 2 sts, dc in next 3 sts, tr in last 4 sts, turn.

Rows 38-41: Repeat row 32 and 37 alternately.

Rows 42-43: (Ch 4, tr) in first st, tr in each st across with 2 tr in last st, turn. At end of last row *(13).*

Rows 44-46: Ch 4, tr next 2 sts tog, tr in each st across to last 2 sts, tr last 2 sts tog, turn. At end of last row *(7).*

Row 47: Ch 4, (tr next 2 sts tog) 2 times, tr in last 2 sts, turn. *(5)*

Row 48: Ch 4, tr next 4 sts tog. Fasten off.

Sew Swan centered on one end of towel, leaving wing and top edge of tail unsewn.

Edging (make 2)
Row 1: Make starting ch to fit across width of towel in multiples of 12 plus 6 at the end, sc in second ch from hook, sc in each ch across, turn.

Row 2: Ch 3, dc in next 4 sts, *ch 3, skip next 3 sts; for **shell (2 dc, ch 2, 2 dc)** in next st; ch 3, skip next 3 sts, dc in next 5 sts; repeat from * across, turn.

Row 3: Sl st in first 2 sts, ch 3, dc in next 2 sts, (ch 4, skip next st, shell in ch sp of next shell, ch 4, skip next st, dc in next 3 sts) across leaving last st unworked, turn.

Row 4: Ch 1, sc in next st, *ch 3, skip next st, sc in next ch sp, ch 3, (2 dc; for **picot, ch 3, sc in 3rd ch from hook;** 2 dc) in next shell, ch 3, sc in next ch sp, ch 3, skip next st, dc in next st; repeat from * across leaving last st unworked. Fasten off.

Sew across each end of towel.

WASHCLOTH
Small Swan
Row 1: Repeat row 1 of Large Swan.

Row 2: Ch 4, 4 tr in first ch-2 sp, skip next 2 sts; for **shell, (2 tr, ch 2, 2 tr)** in next ch sp; ch 3, shell in last ch sp, turn.

Row 3: Ch 4, shell in ch sp of first shell, ch 3, shell in ch sp of next shell, tr in last 5 sts, turn.

Row 4: Ch 4, tr in next 4 sts, ch 3, shell in next shell, 5 dc in next ch-3 sp, shell in last shell, turn.

Row 5: Ch 4, shell in first shell, ch 3, dc in next 5 sts, ch 3, shell in last shell leaving remaining sts unworked, turn.

Row 6: Ch 4, shell in first shell, ch 4, dc in next 5 sts, ch 4, shell in last shell, turn.

Row 7: Ch 4, shell in first shell, ch 5, skip next st, dc in next 3 sts, ch 5, shell in last shell, turn.

Row 8: Ch 4, shell in first shell, ch 5, skip next st, dc in next st, ch 5, shell in last shell, turn.

Row 9: Ch 4, shell in first shell, ch 3, sc in next st, ch 3, shell in last shell, turn.

Rows 10-11: Repeat rows 25-26 of Large Swan.

Row 12: For **neck,** join with sl st

in top of -h 4 on row 4, (ch 4, tr) in same st, tr in next st, dc in next 2 sts, 2 sc in last st, turn. *(7 sts)*

Row 13: Ch 4, tr next 2 sts tog, tr in next 2 sts, tr last sts tog, turn. *(5)*

Row 14: Ch 1, sc in first st, dc in next 2 sts, tr in each of last 2 sts, turn.

Row 15: Ch 4, tr in each st across, turn.

Row 16: Repeat row 14.

Row 17: Ch 4, tr in next st, dc in next 2 sts, sc in last st, turn.

Rows 18-19: Repeat rows 14 and 17.

Row 20: (Ch 4, tr) in first st, tr in each of next 3 sts, 2 tr in last st, turn. *(7)*

Row 21: Ch 4, tr next 2 sts tog, tr in next st, tr last 3 sts tog, turn. *(4)*

Row 22: Ch 3, dc last 3 sts tog. Fasten off. Leaving top body unsewn, sew to corner of washcloth.

Edging
Row 1: Make starting ch to fit around washcloth in multiples of 12 plus 1 at the end, sc in second ch from hook, sc in each ch across, turn.

Row 2: Ch 3, dc in next 2 sts, ch 3, skip next 3 sts; for **shell (2 dc, ch 2, 2 dc)** in next st; (ch 3, skip next 3 sts, dc in next 5 sts, ch 3, skip next 3 sts, shell in next st) across to last 5 sts, ch 3, skip next 3 sts, dc in last 2 sts, turn.

Row 3: Ch 7, skip next st, shell in next shell, (ch 4, skip next st, dc in each of next 3 sts, ch 4, skip next st, shell in next shell) across to last 3 sts, ch 4, skip next st, dc in last 2 sts, turn.

Row 4: Ch 1, sc in first st, ch 3, skip next st, sc in next ch sp, ch 3, (2 dc; for **picot, ch 3, sc in third ch from hook;** 2 dc) in next shell, *ch 3, sc in next ch sp, ch 3, skip next st, sc in next st, ch 3, skip next st, sc in next ch sp, ch 3, (2 dc, picot, 2 dc) in next shell; repeat from * across to ch 7, ch 3, sl st in third ch of ch-7. Fasten off.

Sew ends of rows tog.

Sew around outer edge of washcloth.❏❏

Bedspread

Designed by Dorothy Moder Frantz

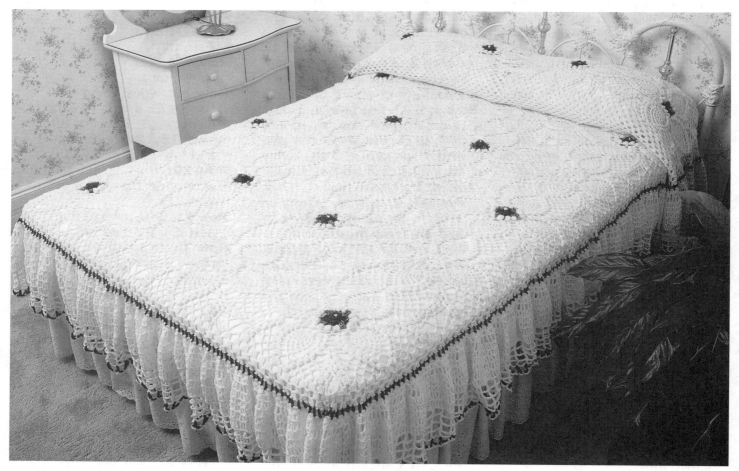

FINISHED SIZE:
Fits 54" x 75" double bed.

MATERIALS:
- 60 oz. yellow pompadour baby yarn
- 4 oz. purple sport yarn
- ⅛" satin ribbon:
    88 yds. purple
    50 yds. green
- Tapestry needle
- G hook or hook size needed to obtain gauge

GAUGE:
Rnds 1-3 of Plain Motif = 3" diameter. One popcorn shell = 1"; 5 popcorn shell rows = 3". 4 dc = 1"; 2 dc rows = 1".

BASIC STITCHES:
Ch, sl st, sc, hdc, dc, tr.

SPECIAL STITCHES:
For **beginning popcorn (beg pc)**, (ch 3, 4 dc) in same sp, drop lp from hook, insert hook in top of ch-3, pull dropped lp through ch.

For **popcorn (pc)**, 5 dc in next ch sp, drop lp from hook, insert hook in top of first dc of group, pull dropped lp through st.

For **beginning popcorn shell (beg pc shell)**, ch 3, 2 dc in first ch sp, drop lp from hook, insert hook in top of ch-3, pull dropped lp through ch, ch 3, 3 dc in same sp, drop lp from hook, insert hook in first dc of group, pull dropped lp through st.

For **popcorn shell (pc shell)**, 3 dc in next ch sp, drop lp from

hook, insert hook in first dc of group, pull dropped lp through st, ch 3, 3 dc in same sp, drop lp from hook, insert hook in first dc of group, pull dropped lp through st.

For **double pc shell (dpc shell)**, 3 dc in next pc shell, drop lp from hook, insert hook in first dc of group, pull dropped lp through st, (ch 3, 3 dc in same pc shell, drop lp from hook, insert hook in first dc of group, pull dropped lp through st) 2 times.

PLAIN MOTIF (make 10)
Rnd 1: With yellow, ch 3, sl st in first ch to form ring, ch 1, 12 sc in ring, join with sl st in first sc. *(12 sc made)*
Rnd 2: Ch 5, (dc in next st, ch 2)

around, join with sl st in third ch of ch-5.

Rnd 3: Sl st in first ch sp, **beg pc** (*see Special Stitches*), ch 3, **pc** (*see Special Stitches*), (ch 3, pc) in each ch sp around, ch 2, join with hdc in top of first sc.

Rnd 4: (Ch 7, sc in next ch-3 sp) 11 times, ch 3, join with tr in top of hdc.

Rnd 5: Beg pc shell (*see Special Stitches*), ch 3, 7 dc in next ch sp, ch 3, **pc shell** (*see Special Stitches*), ch 3, (pc shell in next ch sp, ch 3, 7 dc in next ch sp, ch 3, pc shell in next ch sp, ch 3) around, join with sl st in top of first pc.

Rnd 6: (Sl st, beg pc shell) in ch sp of first pc shell, *[ch 3, skip next ch-3 sp, (dc in next dc, ch 1) 6 times, dc in next dc, ch 3, pc shell in ch sp of next pc shell, ch 5], pc shell in next pc shell; repeat from * 2 more times; repeat between [ ], join.

Rnd 7: (Sl st, beg pc shell) in first pc shell, *[ch 3, skip next ch-3 sp, (sc in next ch-1 sp, ch 3) 6 times, pc shell in next pc shell, ch 7], pc shell in next pc shell; repeat from * 2 more times; repeat between [ ], join.

Rnd 8: (Sl st, beg pc shell) in first pc shell, *[ch 3, skip next ch-3 sp, (sc in next ch-3 sp, ch 3) 5 times, pc shell in next pc shell, ch 5, pc shell in next ch-7 sp, ch 5], pc shell in next pc shell; repeat from * 2 more times; repeat between [ ], join.

Rnd 9: (Sl st, beg pc shell) in first pc shell, *[ch 3, skip next ch-3 sp, (sc in next ch-3 sp, ch 3) 4 times, (pc shell in next pc shell, ch 7) 2 times], pc shell in next pc shell; repeat from * 2 more times; repeat between [ ], join.

Rnd 10: (Sl st, beg pc shell) in first pc shell, *[ch 3, skip next ch-3 sp, (sc in next ch-3 sp, ch 3) 3 times, pc shell in next pc shell, ch 5, sc in next ch-7 sp, ch 5, **dpc shell** (*see Special Stitches*), ch 5, sc in next ch-7 sp, ch 5], pc shell in next pc shell; repeat from * 2 more times; repeat between [ ], join.

Rnd 11: (Sl st, beg pc shell) in first

pc shell, *[ch 3, skip next ch-3 sp, (sc in next ch-3 sp, ch 3) 2 times, pc shell in next pc shell, ch 5, (sc in next ch-5 sp, ch 5) 2 times, pc shell in first ch sp of next dpc shell, ch 2, pc shell in next ch sp of same dpc shell, ch 5, (sc in next ch-5 sp, ch 5) 2 times], pc shell in next pc shell; repeat from * 2 more times; repeat between [ ], join.

Rnd 12: (Sl st, beg pc shell) in first pc shell, *[ch 3, skip next ch-3 sp, sc in next ch-3 sp, ch 3, pc shell in next pc shell, ch 5, (sc in next ch-5 sp, ch 5) 2 times, skip next ch-5 sp, pc shell in next pc shell, ch 5, sc in next ch-2 sp, ch 5, pc shell in next pc shell, ch 5, skip next ch-5 sp, (sc in next ch-5 sp, ch 5) 2 times], pc shell in next pc shell; repeat from * 2 more times; repeat between [ ], join.

Rnd 13: (Sl st, beg pc shell) in first pc shell, *[ch 1, pc shell in next pc shell, ch 5, (sc in next ch-5 sp, ch 5) 3 times, pc shell in next pc shell, ch 5, sc in next ch-5 sp, ch 11, sc in next ch-5 sp, ch 5, pc shell in next pc shell, ch 5, (sc in next ch-5 sp, ch 5) 3 times], pc shell in next pc shell; repeat from * 2 more times; repeat between [ ], join. Fasten off.

FLOWER MOTIF (make 14)

Rnd 1: Hold one strand each purple ribbon and purple yarn together as one, ch 5, sl st in first ch to form ring, ch 1, (sc in ring; for **petal,** ch 4, sc in fourth ch from hook) 4 times, join with sl st in first sc. (*4 petals made*)

Rnd 2: Working in **back lps** (*see Stitch Guide*), ch 1, sc in first sc, ch 2; working behind petals, (sc in next sc between petals, ch 2) 3 times, join. (*4 ch sps*)

Rnd 3: Ch 1, sc in first st, ch 3, (sc in next st, ch 3) 3 times, join.

Rnd 4: (Sl st, ch 1, sc, ch 1, 3 dc, ch 1, sc) in first ch sp, (sc, ch 1, 3 dc, ch 1, sc) in each ch sp around, join. Fasten off.

Rnd 5: Join green ribbon with (sl st, ch 3, 2 dc) in first st, *[ch 3, sc in center st of next 3-dc group, ch 3], skip next ch-1

sp, skip next sc, 3 dc in next sc; repeat from * 2 more times; repeat between [ ], join with sl st in top of ch-3. Fasten off.

Rnd 6: Join yellow with (sl st, beg pc) in first ch-3 sp, *ch 3, pc in next sc, (ch 3, pc) in each of next 2 ch sps; repeat from * 2 more times, ch 3, pc in next sc, ch 3, pc in next ch sp, ch 2, join with hdc in top of beg pc.

Rnds 7-16: Repeat rnds 4-13 of Plain Motif.

For **center of flower,** cut three strands yellow each 6" long. With all strands held together, insert hook in one lp of any st at center of rnd 1, pull ends through lp; with both ends on front, tie in double knot. Trim ends ¼" from knot.

ASSEMBLY

With yellow, working in ch sps only, matching two Motifs together, weaving yarn through chs and sts as you work, (starting at ch-11 of each square, tack together at center ch, *tack ch-5 sps together at edge of pc shell, tack ch-3 sps between pc shells together, tack ch-5 sps together at edge of pc shell, tack center ch on each of next 3 ch-5 sps together*, (tack ch-3 sps of next pc shell together) 2 times; repeat between **, tack ch-3 of next pc shell together, tack ch-5 sp together at edge of pc shell, tack center ch of ch-11 together]; repeat between [ ] according to assembly diagram.

Flower	Plain	Plain	Flower
Plain	Flower	Flower	Plain
Flower	Plain	Plain	Flower
Plain	Flower	Flower	Plain
Flower	Plain	Plain	Flower

PILLOW COVER SECTION

Sew four Flower Motifs together to form one row.

Top Trim

Row 1: With right side facing you, join yellow with (sl st, ch 3, 2 dc) in ch-11 sp at one end of one long edge on Pillow Cover Section; skipping ch sp of each pc shell, (ch 2, 3 dc) in each ch sp and in sp between 2 pc shells at top of each pineapple across with last 3 dc in opposite ch-11 sp, turn.

Row 2: Ch 5, 3 dc in first ch sp, (ch 2, 3 dc) in each ch sp across, ch 2, dc in last st, turn.

Row 3: Ch 3, 2 dc in first ch sp, (ch 2, 3 dc) in each ch sp across, turn.

Rows 4-13: Repeat rows 2 and 3 alternately. At end of last row, fasten off.

Bottom Trim

Rows 1-10: Working on opposite side of Pillow Cover Section, repeat rows 1-10 of Top Trim. At end of last row, fasten off.

Matching 3 sts to each ch sp, sew sts of row 10 to top edge of Bedspread.

RIGHT SIDE TRIM

Row 1: With right side facing you, working in ch sps on Motifs and in ch-5 sps at ends of rows on Pillow Cover Section, join yellow with (sl st, ch 3, 2 dc) in ch-11 sp on Motif at bottom right corner; skipping ch sp of each pc shell, (ch 2, 3 dc) in each ch sp and in sp between pc shells at top of each pineapple across, turn. *(89 dc groups made)*

Row 2: Ch 5, 3 dc in first ch sp, (ch 2, 3 dc) in each ch sp across, ch 2, dc in last st, turn.

Row 3: Ch 3, 2 dc in first ch sp, (ch 2, 3 dc) in each ch sp across, **do not turn.** Fasten off.

Row 4: Join purple with sl st in top of ch-3, ch 5, dc in next st, ch 2, skip next st, dc in next ch sp, ch 2, (skip next st, dc in next st, ch 2, dc in next ch sp, ch 2) across to last 3 sts, skip next st, dc in next st, ch 2, dc in last st, turn. Fasten off. *(179 dc)*

Row 5: Join yellow with (sl st, ch 3, 2 dc) in first ch sp, (ch 1, 3 dc) in each ch sp across, turn.

Row 6: Ch 4, 3 dc in each ch sp across, ch 1, dc in last st, turn.

Row 7: Ch 6, (skip next ch sp, tr in next st, ch 2, skip next st, tr in next st, ch 2) across to ch-4, tr in third ch of ch-4, turn. *(356 tr)*

Rows 8-12: Ch 6, tr in first ch sp; for V st (tr, ch 2, tr) in next ch sp; V st in each ch sp across, turn. *(355 V sts)*

Row 13: Ch 8, skip first V st, tr in sp between next 2 V sts, (ch 5, skip next V st, tr in sp between next 2 V sts) across to last 3 V sts, ch 5, skip next V st, tr in ch sp of next V st, ch 5, tr in fourth ch of ch-6, turn.

Rows 14-15: Ch 8, (tr in next tr, ch 5) across, tr in fourth ch of ch-8, turn.

Row 16: Ch 8, *(tr in next tr, ch 5) 3 times, sc in next tr; repeat from * across to last tr and ch sp, ch 5, tr in last tr, ch 5, tr in fourth ch of ch-8, **do not turn.** Fasten off.

Row 17: Join purple with sl st in fourth ch of ch-8, *(tr in next tr, ch 5) 3 times, sc in next sc; repeat from * across to last 2 tr, ch 5, tr in next tr, ch 5, tr in last tr, **do not turn.** Fasten off.

Row 18: Join yellow with sl st in fourth ch of ch-8, ch 3, sc in first ch sp, ch 3, sc in next st, (ch 3, sc in next ch sp, ch 3, sc in next st) across. Fasten off.

LEFT SIDE TRIM

Row 1: Joining in ch sp at end of row 12 on Pillow Cover Section Top Trim, repeat row 1 of Right Side Trim.

Rows 2-18: Repeat rows 2-18 of Right Side Trim.

END TRIM

Row 1: With right side facing you, working in ch sps on Motifs, join yellow with (sl st, ch 3, 2 dc) in ch-11 sp at bottom right corner; skipping ch sp of each pc shell, (ch 2, 3 dc) in each ch sp and in each sp between pc shells at top of each pineapple across, turn. *(52 dc groups made)*

Rows 2-15: Repeat rows 2-15 of Right side Trim. At end of last row *(105 tr).*

Row 16: Ch 8, tr in next tr, ch 5, sc in next tr, *(ch 5, tr in next tr) 3 times, ch 5, sc in next tr; repeat from * across to last ch sp, ch 5, tr in fourth ch of ch-8, **do not turn.** Fasten off.

Row 17: Join purple with sl st in fourth ch of ch-8, ch 8, tr in next tr, ch 5, sc in next sc, *(ch 5, tr in next tr) 3 times, ch 5, sc in next sc; repeat from * across to last tr, ch 5, tr in last tr, **do not turn.** Fasten off.

Row 18: Join yellow with sl st in fourth ch of ch-8, ch 3, sc in first ch sp, ch 3, sc in next st, (ch 3, sc in next ch sp, ch 3, sc in next st) across. Fasten off.❑❑

Coverlet

Designed by Sister Mary Strecker

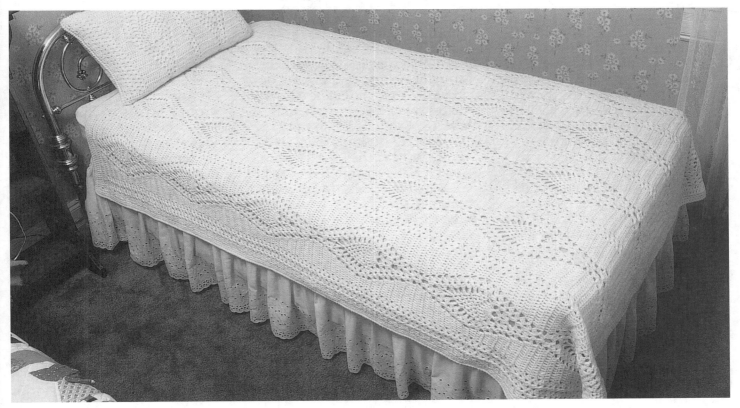

FINISHED SIZE:
Coverlet is 58½" x 74". Pillow is 17" x 27".

MATERIALS:
- 72 oz. worsted yarn.
- 1 yd. muslin fabric
- Sewing thread and needle
- Polyester fiberfill
- H hook or hook size needed to obtain gauge

GAUGE:
7 dc = 2"; 5 dc rows = 3".

BASIC STITCHES:
Ch, sl st, sc, hdc, dc.

SPECIAL STITCHES:
For **shell**, (2 dc, ch 2, 2 dc) in specified st.

For **beginning pattern (beg pat)**, ch 3, dc in next 2 sts, shell in ch sp of next 2 shells.

For **end pattern (end pat),** shell in ch sp of last shell, dc in last 3 sts.

COVERLET

Row 1: Ch 169, dc in fourth ch from hook, dc in each ch across, turn. *(167 dc made)*

Row 2: Ch 3, dc in each st across, turn.

Row 3: Ch 3, dc in next 2 sts, skip next 2 sts, **shell** *(see Special Stitches)* in next st, skip next 2 sts, *shell in next st, skip next 2 sts, dc in next 6 sts, ch 1, skip next 2 sts, shell in next st, skip next 3 sts, (2 dc, ch 4, 2 dc) in next st, skip next 3 sts, shell in next st, ch 1, skip next 2 sts, dc in next 6 sts, skip next 2 sts; repeat from * across to last 9 sts, (shell in next st, skip next 2 sts) 2 times, dc in last 3 sts, turn.

Row 4: Beg pat *(see Special Stitches)*, *dc in next 6 sts, ch 1, shell in ch sp of next shell, 8 dc in next ch-4 sp, shell in next shell, ch 1, dc in next 6 sts, shell

in ch sp of next shell; repeat from * across to last shell, **end pat** *(see Special Stitches,* turn.

Row 5: Beg pat, *dc in next 4 sts, dc next 2 sts tog, ch 1, shell in next shell, (dc in next st, ch 1) 7 times, dc in next st, shell in next shell, ch 1, dc next 2 sts tog, dc in next 4 sts, shell in next shell; repeat from * across to last shell, end pat, turn.

Row 6: Beg pat, *dc in next 3 sts, dc next 2 sts tog, ch 1, shell in next shell, ch 1, sc in next st, (ch 3, sc in next st) 7 times, ch 1, shell in next shell, ch 1, dc next 2 sts tog, dc in next 3 sts, shell in next shell; repeat from * across to last shell, end pat, turn.

Row 7: Beg pat, *dc in next 4 sts, ch 1, shell in next shell, ch 2, sc in next ch-3 sp, (ch 3, sc in next ch-3 sp) 6 times, ch 2, shell in next shell, ch 1, dc in next 4 sts, shell in next shell; repeat from * across to last shell, end pat, turn.

Row 8: Beg pat, *dc in next 4

sts, ch 1, shell in next shell, (ch 3, sc in next ch-3 sp) 6 times, ch 3, shell in next shell, ch 1, dc in next 4 sts, shell in next shell; repeat from * across to last shell, end pat, turn.

Row 9: Beg pat, *dc in next 3 sts, 2 dc in next st, ch 1, shell in next shell, ch 3, skip next ch-3 sp, (sc in next ch-3 sp, ch 3) 5 times, shell in next shell, ch 1, 2 dc in next st, dc in next 3 sts, shell in next shell; repeat from * across to last shell, end pat, turn.

Row 10: Beg pat, *dc in next 4 sts, 2 dc in next st, ch 1, shell in next shell, ch 3, skip next ch-3 sp, (sc in next ch-3 sp, ch 3) 4 times, shell in next shell, ch 1, 2 dc in next st, dc in next 4 sts, shell in next shell; repeat from * across to last shell, end pat, turn.

Row 11: Beg pat, *dc in next 5 sts, 2 dc in next st, ch 1, shell in next shell, ch 3, skip next ch-3 sp, (sc in next ch-3 sp, ch 3) 3 times, shell in next shell, ch 1, 2 dc in next st, dc in next 5 sts, shell in next shell; repeat from * across to last shell, end pat, turn.

Row 12: Beg pat, *dc in next 6 sts, 2 dc in next st, ch 1, shell in next shell, ch 3, skip next ch-3 sp, (sc in next ch-3 sp, ch 3) 2 times, shell in next shell, ch 1, 2 dc in next st, dc in next 6 sts, shell in next shell; repeat from * across to last shell, end pat, turn.

Row 13: Beg pat, *dc in next 7 sts, 2 dc in next st, ch 1, shell in next shell, ch 4, skip next ch-3 sp, sc in next ch-3 sp, ch 4, shell in next shell, ch 1, 2 dc in next st, dc in next 7 sts, shell in next shell; repeat from * across to last shell, end pat, turn.

Row 14: Beg pat, *dc in next 8 sts, 2 dc in next st, ch 1, shell in next shell, dc in next 2 ch-4 sps, shell in next shell, ch 1, 2 dc in next st, dc in next 8 sts, shell in next shell; repeat from * across to last shell, end pat, turn.

Row 15: Beg pat, *dc in next 9 sts, 2 dc in next st, ch 1, (shell in next shell, ch 1) 2 times, 2 dc in next st, dc in next 9 sts, shell in

next shell; repeat from * across to last shell, end pat, turn.

Row 16: Beg pat, (dc in next 10 sts, 2 dc in next st, ch 1, 2 dc in next shell, ch 2, 2 dc in next shell, ch 1, 2 dc in next st, dc in next 10 sts, shell in next shell) across to last shell, end pat, turn.

Row 17: Beg pat, (dc in next 12 sts, ch 1, shell in next ch-2 sp, ch 1, dc in next 12 sts, shell in next shell) across to last shell, end pat, turn.

Row 18: Beg pat, *dc in next 12 sts, ch 1, (2 dc, ch 2, 2 dc, ch 2, 2 dc) in next shell, ch 1, dc in next 12 sts, shell in next shell; repeat from * across to last shell, end pat, turn.

Row 19: Beg pat, *dc in next 10 sts, dc next 2 sts tog, ch 1, shell in next 2 ch-2 sps, ch 1, dc next 2 sts tog, dc in next 10 sts, shell in next shell; repeat from * across to last shell, end pat, turn.

Row 20: Beg pat, *dc in next 9 sts, dc next 2 sts tog, ch 1, (shell in next shell, ch 1) 2 times, dc next 2 sts tog, dc in next 9 sts, shell in next shell; repeat from * across to last shell, end pat, turn.

Row 21: Beg pat, *dc in next 8 sts, dc next 2 sts tog, ch 1, shell in next shell, ch 2, shell in next shell, ch 1, dc next 2 sts tog, dc in next 8 sts, shell in next shell; repeat from * across to last shell, end pat, turn.

Row 22: Beg pat, (dc in next 7 sts, dc next 2 sts tog, ch 1, shell in next shell, shell in next ch-2 sp, shell in next shell, ch 1, dc next 2 sts tog, dc in next 7 sts, shell in next shell) across to last shell, end pat, turn.

Row 23: Beg pat, *dc in next 6 sts, dc next 2 sts tog, ch 1, shell in next shell, (2 dc, ch 4, 2 dc) in next shell, shell in next shell, ch 1, dc next 2 sts tog, dc in next 6 sts, shell in next shell; repeat from * across to last shell, end pat, turn.

Row 24: Beg pat, (dc in next 5 sts, dc next 2 sts tog, ch 1, shell in next shell, 8 dc in next ch-4 sp, shell in next shell, ch 1, dc next 2 sts tog, dc in next 5 sts, shell in next shell) across to last shell, end pat, turn.

Rows 25-115: Repeat rows 5-24 consecutively, ending with row 15.

Row 116: Ch 3, dc in next 2 sts, dc in next 2 dc on first shell, 2 dc in ch sp of same shell, dc in sp between first 2 shells, 3 dc in ch sp of next shell, *dc in next 10 sts, 2 dc in next st, 2 dc in next shell, ch 2, 2 dc in next shell, 2 dc in next st, dc in next 10 sts, 3 dc in next shell; repeat from * across to last shell, dc in sp between last 2 shells, 2 dc in last shell, dc in next 2 dc of same shell, dc in last 3 sts, turn. *(174)*

Row 117: Ch 3, dc in each dc across with dc in each ch-2 sp, turn. *(179)*

Row 118: Ch 3, dc in next 14 sts, dc next 2 sts tog, (dc in next 16 sts, dc next 2 sts tog) across, turn. *(169)*

Row 119: Ch 3, dc in each st across, **do not turn.**

Rnd 120: For **border,** working around outer edge in ends of rows and in sts, ch 2, (2 hdc in each row across to last row, 3 hdc in last row); working in sps between sts on opposite side of starting ch, hdc in each sp across; repeat between ( ), hdc in each sp across, join with sl st in top of ch-2.

Rnds 121-122: Working in sps between sts, ch 2, hdc in each sp around with 3 hdc in each corner sp, join.

Rnd 123: Ch 1; for reverse sc *(see illustration)*, working from left to right, insert hook in top of next st, complete as sc; reverse sc in each st around, join with sl st in first sc. Fasten off.

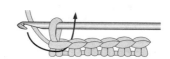

PILLOW SIDE (make 2)
Row 1: Ch 87, dc in fourth ch from hook, dc in each ch across, turn. *(85 dc made)*

Row 2: Ch 3, dc in each st across, turn.

Row 3: Ch 3, dc in next 2 sts, skip next 2 sts, shell in next st, skip next 2 sts, shell in next st, (skip next 2 sts, dc in next 12 sts, ch 1, skip next 2 sts, shell in next st, ch 1, skip next 2 sts, dc in next 12 sts, skip next 2 sts, shell in next st) across to last 8 sts, skip next 2 sts, shell in next st, skip next 2 sts, dc in last 3 sts, turn.

Row 4: Beg pat, *dc in next 12 sts, ch 1, (2 dc, ch 2, 2 dc, ch 2, 2 dc) in next shell, ch 1, dc in next 12 sts, shell in next shell; repeat from * around to last shell, end pat, turn.

Rows 5-10: Repeat rows 19-24 of Coverlet.

Rows 11-23: Repeat rows 5-17 of Coverlet.

Row 24: Ch 3, dc in each dc across with dc in each ch-2 sp, turn. *(89)*

Row 25: Ch 3, dc in next 16 sts, (dc next 2 sts tog, dc in next 16 sts) across, **do not turn.** *(85)*

Rnd 26: Working around outer edge in ends of rows and in sts, ch 2, (2 hdc in each row across to last row, 3 hdc in last row); working in sps between sts on opposite side of starting ch, hdc in each sp across; repeat between ( ), hdc in each sp across, join with sl st in top of ch-2. Fasten off.

Pillow Form

From fabric, using Pillow Side for pattern, cut two pieces ¾" larger on all edges. Allowing ¼" for seam, sew right sides together leaving 6" open for turning. Clip corners. Turn. Stuff. Sew opening closed.

Assembly

With Pillow Sides wrong sides together, working around outer edge through both thicknesses, join with sl st in any st, ch 1, reverse sc in each st around, inserting Pillow Form before closing, join with sl st in first sc. Fasten off.❑❑

Oval Tablecloth

Designed by Agnes Russell

FINISHED SIZE:
57" x 65".

MATERIALS:
❑ 3400 yds. size 10 crochet cotton thread

❑ No. 7 steel hook or hook size needed to obtain gauge

GAUGE:
2 shells = 1¼"; 2 shell rows = ¾".

BASIC STITCHES:
Ch, sl st, sc, hdc, dc.

SPECIAL STITCHES:
For **beginning shell (beg shell)**, sl st in next st, (sl st, ch 3, dc, ch 3, 2 dc) in first ch sp.

For **shell**, (2 dc, ch 3, 2 dc) in specified st.

For **pineapple (p-apl)**, ch 3, skip next ch-3 sp, (sc in next ch sp, ch 3) across pineapple, skip next ch-3 sp.

TABLECLOTH

Rnd 1: Ch 64, dc in fourth ch from hook, (ch 3, 2 dc) 3 times in same ch, [skip next 4 chs, **shell** *(see Special Stitches)* in next ch] 11 times, skip next 4 chs, (shell, ch 3, shell) in last ch; working on opposite side of ch, repeat between [ ] 11 times, skip last 4 chs, join with sl st in top of ch-3. *(26 shells made)*

Rnd 2: Beg shell *(see Special Stitches)*, (shell, ch 3, shell) in next ch sp, shell in ch sp of next 13 shells, (shell, ch 3, shell) in next ch sp, shell in ch sp of last 12 shells, join. *(30 shells)*

Rnd 3: Beg shell, shell in next shell, (shell, ch 3, shell) in next ch sp, shell in next 15 shells, (shell, ch 3, shell) in next ch sp, shell in last 13 shells, join. *(34 shells)*

Rnd 4: Beg shell, ch 1, (shell, ch 1) in next 2 shells, shell in next ch sp, ch 1, (shell, ch 1) in next 17 shells, shell in next ch sp, ch 1, (shell, ch 1) in last 14 shells, join. *(36 shells)*

Rnd 5: Beg shell, ch 2, (shell, ch 2) in each shell around, join.

Rnd 6: Beg shell, ch 3, (shell, ch 3) in each shell around, join.

Rnd 7: Beg shell, ch 3, (2 dc, ch 5, 2 dc) in next shell, ch 3, *shell in next shell, ch 3, (2 dc, ch 5, 2 dc) in next shell, ch 3; repeat from * around, join.

Rnd 8: Beg shell, (*ch 3, skip next ch-3 sp; to place pineapple, 8 dc in next ch-5 sp; ch 3, skip next ch-3 sp*, shell in next shell) 17 times; repeat between **, join. *(18 shells, 144 dc)*

Rnd 9: Beg shell, *[ch 3, skip next ch-3 sp, dc in next dc, (ch 1, dc in next dc) across pineapple, ch 3, skip next ch-3 sp], shell in next shell; repeat from * 16 more times; repeat between [ ], join.

Rnd 10: Beg shell; *p-apl *(see Special Stitches,* shell in next shell; repeat from * 16 more times; p-apl, join.

Rnd 11: Beg shell, ch 3, 2 dc in same sp, *p-apl, (shell, ch 3, 2 dc) in next shell; repeat from * 16 more times, p-apl, join.

Rnd 12: Beg shell, shell in next ch sp, (p-apl, shell in next 2 ch sps) 17 times, p-apl, join.

Rnd 13: Beg shell, (*dc in sp between shells, shell in next shell, p-apl*, shell in next shell) 17 times; repeat between **, join.

Rnd 14: Beg shell, (*ch 3, shell in next dc, ch 3, shell in next shell, p-apl*, shell in next shell) 17 times; repeat between **, join.

Rnd 15: Beg shell, *[ch 3, (2 dc, ch 5, 2 dc) in next shell, ch 3, shell in next shell, p-apl], shell in next shell; repeat from * 16 more times; repeat between [ ], join.

Rnd 16: Beg shell, (*ch 3, skip next ch-3 sp; to place pineap-ple, 10 dc in next ch-5 sp; ch 3, skip next ch-3 sp, shell in next shell, ch 3, skip next ch-3 sp, sc in next ch-3 sp, ch 3, skip next ch-3 sp*, shell in next shell) 17 times; repeat between **, join.

Rnd 17: Beg shell, *[ch 3, skip next ch-3 sp, dc in next dc, (ch 1, dc in next dc) across pineapple, ch 3, skip next ch-3 sp, shell in next shell, dc in next sc], shell in next shell; repeat from * 16 more times; repeat between [ ], join.

Rnds 18-19: Beg shell, *(p-apl, shell in next 2 shells) 17 times, p-apl, shell in last shell, join.

Rnd 20: Beg shell, (p-apl, shell in next shell, dc in sp between shells, shell in next shell) 17 times, p-apl, shell in last shell, dc in sp between shells, join.

Rnd 21: Beg shell, (p-apl, shell in next shell, shell in next dc, shell in next shell) 17 times, p-apl, shell in next shell, shell in last dc, join.

Rnds 22-23: Beg shell, *p-apl, shell in next shell, (ch 3, shell in next shell) across to next pine-apple; repeat from * 16 more times, p-apl, (shell in next shell, ch 3) across, join.

Rnd 24: Beg shell, *[p-apl, shell in next shell, ch 3, (2 dc, ch 6, 2 dc) in next shell, ch 3], shell in next shell; repeat from * 16 more times; repeat between [ ], join.

Rnd 25: Beg shell, (*p-apl, shell in next shell, ch 3, skip next ch-3 sp; to place pineapple, 12 dc in next ch-6 sp; ch 3, skip next ch-3 sp*, shell in next shell) 17 times; repeat between **, join.

Rnd 26: Beg shell, *[p-apl, shell in next shell, ch 3, skip next ch-3 sp, dc in next dc, (ch 1, dc in next dc) across pineapple, ch 3, skip next ch-3 sp], shell in next shell; repeat from * 16 more times; repeat between [ ], join.

Rnd 27: Beg shell, (*dc in next sc, shell in next shell, p-apl*, shell in next shell) 17 times; repeat between **, join.

Rnd 28: Beg shell, (*skip next dc, shell in next shell, p-apl*, shell in next shell) 17 times; repeat between **, join.

Rnd 29: Beg shell, (*shell in next shell, p-apl*, shell in next shell) 17 times; repeat between **, join.

Rnd 30: Beg shell, (*dc in sp between shells, shell in next shell, p-apl*, shell in next shell) 17 times; repeat between **, join.

Rnd 31: Beg shell, (*shell in next dc, shell in next shell, p-apl*, shell in next shell) 17 times; repeat between **, join.

Rnds 32-33: Beg shell, *(ch 3, shell in next shell) 2 times, p-apl, shell in next shell; repeat from * 16 more times, (ch 3, shell in next shell) 2 times, p-apl, join.

Rnd 34: Beg shell, (*ch 3, shell in next shell, ch 3, 2 dc in same shell, ch 3, shell in next shell, p-apl*, shell in next shell) 17 times; repeat between **, join.

Rnd 35: Beg shell, (*ch 3, skip next ch-3 sp, shell in each of next 2 ch-3 sps, ch 3, shell in next shell, p-apl*, shell in next shell) 17 times; repeat between **, join.

Rnd 36: Beg shell, (*ch 3, shell in next shell, ch 1, dc in sp between shells, ch 1, shell in next shell, ch 3, shell in next shell, p-apl*, shell in next shell) 17 times; repeat between **, join.

Rnd 37: Beg shell, (*ch 3, shell in next shell, shell in next dc, shell in next shell, ch 3, shell in next shell, p-apl*, shell in next shell) 17 times; repeat between **, join.

Rnd 38: Beg shell, *(ch 3, shell in next shell) 4 times, dc in next sc, shell in next shell; repeat from * 16 more times, (ch 3, shell in next shell) 4 times, dc in next sc, join.

Rnd 39: Beg shell, *[ch 3, shell in next shell, ch 3, (shell, ch 3, 2 dc) in next shell, (ch 3, shell in next shell) 2 times, skip next dc], shell in next shell; repeat from * 16 more times; repeat between [ ], join.

Rnd 40: Beg shell, *[ch 3, shell in next shell, ch 3, skip next ch-3 sp, shell in next 2 ch-3 sps, (ch 3, shell in next shell) 2 times], shell in next shell; repeat from * 16 more times; repeat between [ ], join.

Rnd 41: Beg shell, *[ch 3, shell in next shell, ch 3, shell in next shell, dc in sp between shells, shell in next shell], (ch 3, shell in next shell) 3 times; repeat from *

16 more times; repeat between [ ], (ch 3, shell in next shell) 2 times, ch 3, join.

Rnd 42: Beg shell, (ch 3, shell in next shell) 2 times, *shell in next dc, shell in next shell, (ch 3, shell in next shell) 5 times; repeat from * 16 more times, shell in next dc, (shell in next shell, ch 3) 3 times, join.

Rnd 43: Beg shell, ch 3, (shell in next shell, ch 3) around, join.

Rnd 44: Beg shell, *[ch 3, (shell in next shell, ch 3) 2 times; to place pineapple, 10 dc in next shell]; (ch 3, shell in next shell) 4 times; repeat from * 16 more times; repeat between [ ], ch 3, (shell in next shell, ch 3) 3 times, join.

Rnd 45: Beg shell, *[ch 3, (shell in next shell, ch 3) 2 times, dc in next dc, (ch 1, dc in next dc) across pineapple], (ch 3, shell in next shell) 4 times; repeat from * 16 more times; repeat between [ ], ch 3, (shell in next shell, ch 3) 3 times, join.

Rnds 46-52: Beg shell, *(ch 3, shell in next shell) across to next pineapple, p-apl, shell in next shell; repeat from * 16 more times, ch 3, (shell in next shell, ch 3) around, join.

Rnd 53: Beg shell, *(ch 4, shell in next shell) across to next pine-apple, p-apl , shell in next shell; repeat from * 16 more times, ch 4, (shell in next shell, ch 4) around, join.

Rnd 54: Beg shell, *(ch 4, shell in next shell) across to next pine-apple, ch 2, dc in pineapple, ch 2, shell in next shell; repeat from * 17 more times, ch 4, (shell in next shell, ch 4) around, join.

Rnd 55: Beg shell, *[ch 4, shell in next shell, ch 4, shell in next shell, ch 2, (dc, ch 3, dc) in next dc, ch 2, (shell in next shell, ch 4) 2 times, shell in next shell, ch 2, (dc, ch 3, dc) in second ch of next ch-4, ch 2], shell in next shell; repeat from * 16 more times; repeat between [ ], join.

Rnd 56: Beg shell, *[ch 4, shell in next shell, ch 4, shell in next shell, ch 3, skip next ch-2 sp, shell in next ch-3 sp, ch 3, (shell in next shell, ch 4) 2 times, shell in next shell, ch 3, skip next ch-2 sp, shell in next ch-3 sp, ch 3], shell in next shell; repeat from * 16 more times; repeat between [ ], join.

Rnd 57: Beg shell, *[ch 4, shell in next shell, ch 4, shell in next shell, ch 3; to place pineapple, 10 dc in next shell; ch 3, shell in next shell], (ch 4, shell in next shell) 4 times; repeat from * 16 more times; repeat between [ ], (ch 4, shell in next shell) 3 times, ch 4, join.

Rnd 58: Beg shell, *[ch 4, shell in next shell, ch 4, shell in next shell, ch 3, dc in next dc, (ch 1, dc in next dc) across pineapple, ch 3, shell in next shell], (ch 4, shell in next shell) 4 times; repeat from * 16 more times; repeat between [ ], ch 4, (shell in next shell, ch 4) 3 times, join.

Rnd 59: Beg shell, *[ch 4, shell in next shell, ch 4, shell in next shell, p-apl, (shell in next shell, ch 4) 3 times, [shell, ch 3, 2 dc) in next shell, ch 4], shell in next shell; repeat from * 16 more times; repeat between [ ], join.

Rnd 60: Beg shell, *[ch 4, shell in next shell, ch 4, shell in next shell, p-apl, (shell in next shell, ch 4) 3 times, skip next ch-4 sp, shell in each of next 2 ch-3 sps, ch 4], shell in next shell; repeat from * 16 more times; repeat between [ ], join.

Rnd 61: Beg shell, *[ch 4, shell in next shell, ch 4, shell in next shell, p-apl, (shell in next shell, ch 4) 3 times, shell in next shell, dc in sp between shells, shell in next shell, ch 4], shell in next shell; repeat from * 16 more times; repeat between [ ], join.

Rnd 62: Beg shell, *[ch 4, shell in next shell, ch 4, shell in next shell, p-apl, (shell in next shell, ch 4) 3 times, shell in next shell, shell in next dc, shell in next shell, ch 4], shell in next shell; repeat from * 16 more times; repeat between [ ], join.

Rnds 63-64: Beg shell, *[ch 4, shell in next shell, ch 4, shell in next shell, p-apl, (shell in next shell, ch 4) 6 times], shell in next shell; repeat from * 16 more times; repeat between [ ], join.

Rnd 65: Beg shell, *[ch 4, shell in next shell, ch 4, shell in next shell, p-apl, (shell in next shell, ch 4) 4 times, (shell, ch 3, 2 dc) in next shell], (ch 4, shell in next shell) 2 times; repeat from * 16 more times; repeat between [ ], ch 4, shell in next shell, ch 4, join.

Rnd 66: Beg shell, *[ch 4, shell in next shell, ch 4, shell in next shell, p-apl, (shell in next shell, ch 4) 4 times, skip next ch-4 sp, shell in each of next 2 ch-3 sps], (ch 4, shell in next shell) 2 times; repeat from * 16 more times; repeat between [ ], ch 4, shell in next shell, ch 4, join.

Rnd 67: Beg shell, *[ch 4, shell in next shell, ch 4, shell in next shell, p-apl, (shell in next shell, ch 4) 4 times, shell in next shell, ch 2, dc in sp between shells, ch 2, shell in next shell], (ch 4, shell in next shell) 2 times; repeat from * 16 more times; repeat between [ ], ch 4, shell in next shell, ch 4, join.

Rnd 68: Beg shell, *[ch 4, shell in next shell, ch 4, shell in next shell, ch 1, dc in next sc, ch 1, (shell in next shell, ch 4) 4 times, shell in next shell, ch 2, shell in next dc, ch 2, shell in next shell], (ch 4, shell in next shell) 2 times; repeat from * 16 more times; repeat between [ ], ch 4, shell in next shell, ch 4, join.

Rnd 69: Beg shell, *[ch 4, shell in next shell, ch 4, shell in next shell, skip next dc, shell in next shell], (ch 4, shell in next shell) 8 times; repeat from * 16 more times; repeat between [ ], ch 4, (shell in next shell, ch 4) around, join.

Rnd 70: Ch 1, sc in each dc, 3 sc in each ch-3 sp and 4 sc in each ch-4 sp around, join with sl st in first sc.

Rnd 71: Ch 2, **hdc front post** (*fp, see Stitch Guide*) around next sc, ***hdc back post (bp)** around next sc, fp around next sc; repeat from * around, join with sl st in top of ch-2. Fasten off.❑❑

Place Mat

Designed by Agnes Russell

FINISHED SIZE:
14" x 18".

MATERIALS:
- ❏ 300 yds. size 10 crochet cotton thread
- ❏ No. 7 steel hook or hook size needed to obtain gauge

GAUGE:
9 sts = 1"; 3 dc rows = 1".

BASIC STITCHES:
Ch, sl st, sc, dc.

SPECIAL STITCHES:
For **beginning shell (beg shell)**, sl st in next st, (sl st, ch 3, dc, ch 3, 2 dc) in first ch sp.

For **shell**, (2 dc, ch 3, 2 dc) in specified st.

PLACE MAT
Rnd 1: Ch 34, dc in fourth ch from hook, (ch 3, 2 dc in same ch) 3 times, *skip next 4 chs, **shell** (see Special Stitches) in next ch*; repeat between ** 4 more times, skip next 4 chs, (shell, ch 3, shell) in last ch; working on opposite side of starting ch; repeat between ** 5 times, skip last 4 chs, join with sl st in top of ch-3. *(14 shells made)*

Rnd 2: Beg shell *(see Special Stitches)*, (shell, ch 3, shell) in next ch sp, shell lin ch sp of next 7 shells, (shell, ch 3, shell) in next ch sp, shell in ch sp of last 6 shell, join. *(18 shells)*

Rnd 3: Beg shell, shell in next shell, (shell, ch 3, shell) in next ch sp, shell in next 9 shells, (shell, ch 3, shell) in next ch sp, shell in next 7 shells, join. *(22 shells)*

Rnd 4: Beg shell, ch 1, (shell, ch 1) in each of next 2 shells, shell in next ch sp, ch 1, (shell, ch 1) in next 11 shells, shell in next ch sp, (ch 1, shell, ch 1) in last 8 shells, join. *(24 shells)*

Rnd 5: Beg shell, ch 2, (shell, ch 2) in each shell around, join.

Rnd 6: Beg shell, ch 3, (shell, ch 3) in each shell around, join.

Rnd 7: Beg shell, ch 3, (2 dc, ch 5, 2 dc) in next shell, ch 3, *shell in next shell, ch 3, (2 dc, ch 5, 2 dc) in next shell, ch 3; repeat from * around, join.

Rnd 8: Beg shell, (*ch 3, skip next ch-3 sp, 8 dc in next ch-5 sp, ch 3, skip next ch-3 sp*, shell in next shell) 11 times; repeat between **, join. *(12 shells 96 dc)*

Rnd 9: Beg shell, *[ch 3, skip next ch-3 sp, dc in next st, (ch 1, dc in next st) 7 times, ch 3, skip next ch-3 sp], shell in next shell; repeat from * 10 more times; repeat between [ ], join.

Rnd 10: Beg shell, *[ch 3, skip next ch-3 sp, (sc in next ch-1 sp, ch 3) 7 times, skip next ch-3 sp], shell in next shell; repeat from * 10 more times; repeat between [ ], join.

Rnd 11: Beg shell, ch 3, 2 dc in same sp, *[ch 3, skip next ch-3 sp, (sc in next ch-3 sp, ch 3) 6 times, skip next ch-3 sp], (shell, ch 3, 2 dc) in next shell; repeat from * 10 more times; repeat between [ ], join.

Rnd 12: Beg shell, shell in next ch sp, *[ch 3, skip next ch-3 sp, (sc in next ch-3 sp, ch 3) 5 times, skip next ch-3 sp], shell in each of next 2 ch sps; repeat from * 10 more times; repeat between [ ], join.

Rnd 13: Beg shell, *[dc in next sp between shells, shell in next shell, ch 3, skip next ch-3 sp, (sc in next ch-3 sp, ch 3) 4 times, skip next ch-3 sp], shell in next shell; repeat from * 10 more times; repeat between [ ], join.

Rnd 14: Beg shell, *[ch 3, shell in next dc, ch 3, shell in next shell, ch 3, skip next ch-3 sp, (sc in next ch-3 sp, ch 3) 3 times, skip next ch-3 sp], shell in next shell; repeat from * 10 more times; repeat between [ ], join.

Rnd 15: Beg shell, *[ch 3, (2 dc, ch 5, 2 dc) in next shell, ch 3, shell in next shell, ch 3, skip next ch-3 sp, (sc in next ch-3 sp, ch 3) 2 times, skip next ch-3 sp, shell in next shell; repeat from * 10 more times; repeat between [ ], join.

Rnd 16: Beg shell, (*ch 3, skip next ch-3 sp, 12 dc in next ch-5 sp, ch 3, skip next ch-3 sp, shell in next shell, ch 3, skip next ch-3 sp, sc in next ch-3 sp, ch 3, skip next ch-3 sp*, shell in next shell) 11 times; repeat between **, join.

Rnd 17: Beg shell, *[ch 3, skip next ch-3 sp, dc in next st, (ch 1, dc in next st) 11 times, ch 3, skip next ch-3 sp, shell in next shell, dc in next sc], shell in next shell; repeat from * 11 more times; repeat between [ ], join.

Rnd 18: Sl st in next st, (sl st, ch 3, 2 dc) in next ch-3 sp, *[dc in next 2 sts, 3 dc in next ch-3 sp, (dc in next st, dc in next ch-1 sp) 11 times, dc in next st, 3 dc in next ch-3 sp, dc in next 2 sts, 3 dc in next ch-3 sp], skip next 5 sts, 3 dc in next ch-3 sp; repeat from * 10 more times; repeat between [ ], join. *(468 dc)*

Rnd 19: Ch 1, sc in each st around, join with sl st in first sc.

Rnd 20: Ch 1, *(sc, ch 3, 2 dc) in next st, skip next 2 sts; repeat from * around, join. Fasten off.❏❏

Earrings

Designed by Lela Gunning

FINISHED SIZE:
3¾" long.

MATERIALS:
❏ 75 yds. size 30 crochet cotton thread
❏ Fabric stiffener or spray starch
❏ 2 ear wires
❏ No. 10 steel hook

BASIC STITCHES:
Ch, sl st, sc, dc.

SPECIAL STITCHES:
For **beginning shell (beg shell),** (ch 3, dc, ch 2, 2 dc) in ch sp of specified shell.

For **shell,** (2 dc, ch 2, 2 dc) in ring or ch sp of specified shell.

PINEAPPLE (make 2)
Row 1: Ch 5, sl st in first ch to form ring, ch 3, (dc, ch 2, 2 dc) in ring *(first shell made)*, *ch 1, **shell** (see Special Stitches) in ring; repeat from * one time, turn.

Row 2: Sl st in first 2 sts, (sl st, **beg shell**—see Special Stitches) in next ch sp, (ch 3, shell in next ch-2 sp) 2 times, turn.

Row 3: Sl st in first 2 sts, (sl st, beg shell) in first shell, ch 2, 10 dc in ch sp of next shell, ch 2, shell in last shell, turn.

Row 4: Sl st in first 2 sts, (sl st, beg shell) in first shell, ch 2, skip next ch sp, dc in next st, (ch 1, dc in next st) 9 times, ch 2, shell in last shell, turn.

Row 5: Sl st in first 2 sts, (sl st, beg shell) in first shell, ch 2, skip next ch-2 sp, sc in next ch-1 sp, (ch 3, sc in next ch-1 sp) 8 times, ch 2, shell in last shell, turn.

Rows 6-8: Sl st in first 2 sts, (sl st, beg shell) in first shell, ch 2, skip next ch-2 sp, sc in first ch-3 sp, (ch 3, sc in next ch-3 sp) across, ch 2, shell in last shell, turn.

Row 9: Sl st in first 2 sts, (sl st, beg shell) in first shell, ch 3, skip next ch-2 sp, sc in first ch-3 sp, (ch 3, sc in next ch-3 sp) across, ch 3, shell in shell, turn.

Row 10: Sl st in first 2 sts, (sl st, beg shell) in first shell, ch 4, skip next ch-3 sp, sc in next ch-3 sp, (ch 3, sc in next ch-3 sp) 3 times, ch 4, shell in last shell, turn.

Row 11: Sl st in first 2 sts, (sl st, beg shell) in first shell, ch 4, skip next ch-4 sp, sc in next ch-3 sp, (ch 3, sc in next ch-3 sp) 2 times, ch 4, shell in last shell, turn.

Row 12: Sl st in first 2 sts, (sl st, beg shell) in first shell, ch 5, skip next ch-4 sp, sc in next ch-3 sp, ch 3, sc in next ch-3 sp, ch 5, shell in last shell, turn.

Row 13: Sl st in first 2 sts, (sl st, beg shell) in first shell, ch 5, skip next ch-4 sp, sc in next ch-3 sp, ch 5, shell in last shell, turn.

Row 14: Sl st in first 2 sts, (sl st, beg shell) in first shell, skip next 2 ch-5 sps, shell in last shell, turn.

Row 15: Sl st in first 2 sts, (sl st, ch 3, dc) in first shell, 2 dc in last shell, turn.

Row 16: Sl st in first 2 sts, (sl st, ch 3, sl st) in next ch sp. Fasten off.

Block and stiffen earrings.

Open loop on bottom of ear wire, insert end in ch-5 ring of row 1, close loop on ear wire.❏❏

Swan Sculpture

Designed by Nancy Weddle

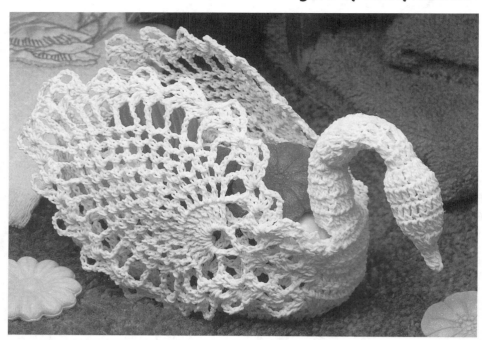

FINISHED SIZE:
4½" tall x 8" long

MATERIALS:
- ❏ 400 yds. size 10 crochet cotton thread
- ❏ 8" of 6mm chenille stem
- ❏ Fabric stiffener
- ❏ Plastic wrap
- ❏ Embroidery needle
- ❏ No. 8 steel hook or hook size needed to obtain gauge

GAUGE:
15 dc = 2", 4 dc rows = 1"; 2 tr rows = ⅞", 5 shell rows = 2".

BASIC STITCHES:
Ch, sl st, sc, dc, tr.

SPECIAL STITCHES:
For **beginning shell (beg shell),** ch 5, (2 dc, ch 3, 2 dc) in ch sp of first shell.

For **shell,** (2 dc, ch 3, 2 dc) in next st.

BODY
Rnd 1: Starting at **bottom,** ch 27, dc in fourth ch from hook, dc in next 22 chs, 5 dc in last ch; working on opposite side of ch, dc in next 22 chs, 3 dc in last ch, join with sl st in top of ch-3. *(54 dc made) First 3 ch counts as first dc.*

Rnd 2: Ch 3, (2 dc in next st, dc in next 22 sts, 2 dc in next st, dc in next st, 3 dc in next st), dc in next st; repeat between ( ), join. *(62)*

Rnd 3: (Ch 3, dc) in first st, dc in next st, 2 dc in next st, *dc in next 22 sts, (2 dc in next st, dc in next st) 2 times, 3 dc in next st*, (dc in next st, 2 dc in next st) 2 times; repeat **, dc in last st, join. *(74)*

Rnd 4: Ch 3, dc in next 3 sts, (2 dc in next st, dc in next 22 sts, 2 dc in next st, dc in next 4 sts, 2 dc in next st, dc in next st, 3 dc in next st, dc in next st, 2 dc in next st) dc in next 4 sts; repeat between ( ), join. *(86)*

Rnd 5: Ch 3, dc in next 37 sts, dc next 2 sts tog, dc in next 41 sts, dc next 2 sts tog, dc in last 3 sts, join. *(84)*

Rnd 6: (Ch 3, dc, ch 3, 2 dc) in first st, skip next 3 sts, *shell (see Special Stitches), skip next 3 sts; repeat from * around, join. *(21 shells)*

Rnds 7-10: Sl st in next st, (sl st, ch 3, dc, ch 3, 2 dc) in next ch sp, (shell in ch sp of next shell) around, join.

Rnd 11: Sl st in next st, (sl st, ch 1, sc) in next ch sp; (for **picot, ch 5, sl st in third ch from hook;** ch 2, sc in next ch sp) around, (picot, ch 2), join with sl st in first sc. Fasten off.

NECK & HEAD
Row 1: Starting at **bottom of Neck,** ch 18, dc in fourth ch from hook, dc in each ch across, turn. *(16 dc made)*

Row 2: Ch 3, dc next 2 sts tog, dc in each st across to last 3 sts, dc next 2 sts tog, dc in last st, turn. *(14)*

Row 3: Ch 3, dc in each st across, turn.

Rows 4-5: Repeat rows 2 and 3. *(12)*

Rnd 6: Working in rnds, repeat row 2, **do not turn,** ch 10, join with sl st in top of ch-3, **turn.** *(10 dc, 10 chs)*

Rnd 7: Ch 3, dc in each ch and in each st around, join. *(20)*

Rnd 8: Ch 3, dc in each st around, join.

Rnd 9: Ch 3, (dc next 2 sts tog, dc in next 3 sts) 3 times, dc next 2 sts tog, dc in last 2 sts, join. *(16)*

Rnds 10-13: Ch 3, dc in each st around, join.

Rnd 14: Ch 3, (dc next 2 sts tog, dc in next st) 5 times, join. *(11)*

Rnds 15-16: Ch 3, dc next 2 sts tog, dc in each st around, join. *(10, 9)*

Rnd 17: Ch 3, dc in each st around, join.

Rnd 18: For **Head,** (ch 3, dc) in first st, 2 dc in each st around, join. *(18)*

Rnds 19-20: Ch 3, dc in each st around, join.

Rnd 21: Ch 3, (dc next 2 st tog, dc in next st) 5 times, dc last 2 sts tog, join. *(12)*

Rnd 22: Ch 2, dc in next st, (dc

next 2 sts tog) around, join with sl st in first dc. *(6) Ch-2 is not counted as a st.*

Rnd 23: Ch 4, *yo 2 times, insert hook in next st, yo, pull through st, (yo, pull through 2 lps on hook) 2 times; repeat from * 4 more times, yo, pull through all 6 lps on hook, ch 1. Fasten off.

WINGS

Row 1: For **first Wing,** with right side facing you, working in ends of rows 1, 3 and 5 on Neck, join with sl st in end of row 1, (ch 3, dc, ch 3, 2 dc) in same row as sl st, (skip next row, shell in next row) 2 times, turn. *(3 shells made)*

Rows 2-3: Beg shell *(see Special Stitches),* shell in each shell across, turn.

Row 4: Beg shell, (ch 2, dc, ch 6, dc, ch 2) in next shell, shell in next shell, turn. *(2 shells, 1 ch-6 sp)*

Row 5: Beg shell, ch 2, 13 tr in ch-6 sp, ch 2, shell in next shell, turn. *(2 shells, 13 tr)*

Row 6: Beg shell, ch 2, tr in first tr, (ch 1, tr in next tr) 12 times, ch 2, shell in next shell, turn.

Rows 7-17: Beg shell, ch 3, skip next ch sp, sc in next ch sp, (ch 3, sc in next ch sp) across to last ch sp, ch 3, skip next ch sp, shell in next shell, turn.

Row 18: Beg shell, ch 3, skip next ch sp, sc in next ch-3 sp, ch 3, skip next ch sp, 2 dc in ch sp of next shell, ch 1, sl st back into ch sp of beg shell on this row, ch 1, 2 dc in same ch sp as last dc, ch 3, sl st in last dc of row 17. Fasten off.

For **second Wing,** working on opposite ends of rows 1, 3 and 5, joining in row 5 and working to row 1, repeat rows 1–18 of first Wing.

FINISHING

Place rows 1-5 of Neck over rows 7-11 at one end of Body, sew in place leaving Wings unsewn.

Cover chenille stem with plastic wrap. Insert in Neck and Head, shape. Soak Swan with fabric stiffener, stuff with plastic wrap; shaping while drying, let dry. Remove chenille stem and plastic wrap.❑❑

Pineapple Lace Afghan

Designed by Carol Alexander

FINISHED SIZE:
43¾" x 60".

MATERIALS:
- ❑ 39 oz. white worsted yarn
- ❑ 4 yds. ⅜" picot-edge satin ribbon
- ❑ 2 large ribbon roses with leaves
- ❑ Sewing and tapestry needles
- ❑ White sewing thread
- ❑ G hook or hook size needed to obtain gauge

GAUGE:
4 hdc = 1"; rows 4-5 = 1".

BASIC STITCHES:
Ch, sl st, sc, hdc, dc, tr.

SPECIAL STITCHES:
For **scallop,** (dc, ch 1, dc, ch 1, dc) in next st or in ch sp of next picot.

For **sc picot (picot),** (sc, ch 3, sc) in next dc or in center dc of next scallop.

For **shell,** (2 dc, ch 2, 2 dc) in st or ch or in ch sp of next shell.

For **edge scallop,** (dc, ch 2, dc, ch 3, sl st in top of last dc made, dc, ch 2, dc) in st or ch-4 sp.

For **joined scallop,** (dc, ch 2, dc, ch 1, sl st in matching ch-3 sp on adjacent Pineapple, ch 1, sl st in top of last dc made, dc, ch 2, dc) in next ch-4 sp.

CENTER
Row 1: Ch 170, hdc in third ch from hook, hdc in each ch across, **do not turn.** Fasten off. *(Ch-2 counts as first hdc-169 hdc made)*
Row 2: Join with sl st in top of ch-2, ch 1, sc in next st, skip next 2 sts, **scallop** *(see Special Stitches)* in next st, skip next 2 sts, (sc in next st, ch 3, sc in next st, skip next 2 sts, scallop in next st, skip next 2 sts) across to last st, sc in last st, turn. *(24 scallops, 23 ch-3 sps, 48 sc)*
Row 3: Ch 7 *(counts as tr and ch-3)*, **picot** *(see Special Stitches)* in next scallop, ch 3, (dc in next ch-3 sp, ch 3, picot in next scallop, ch 3) across to last sc, tr in last sc leaving ch-1 and sl st unworked, turn *(24 picots, 23 dc, 2 tr)*
Row 4: Ch 1, sc in first st, skip next ch-3, scallop in next picot, skip next ch-3, (picot in next dc, skip next ch-3, scallop in next picot, skip next ch-3) across to last st, sc in last st, turn. *(24 scallops, 23 picots, 2 sc)*
Row 5: Ch 7, picot in next scallop, ch 3, (dc in next picot, ch 3, picot in next scallop, ch 3) across to last sc, tr in last sc, turn. *(24 picots, 23 dc, 2 tr)*
Rows 6-84: Repeat rows 4 and 5 alternately, ending with row 4. At end of last row, **do not turn.** Fasten off.
Row 85: Join with sl st in first sc, (ch 2, hdc) in same st as sl st; skipping each ch-3 sp, hdc

in each st and in each ch-1 sp across. Fasten off. *(169 hdc)*

Border (make 2)
First Section
Row 1: For **Base,** ch 10, dc in seventh ch from hook *(counts as 2 dc and ch-2 sp)*, ch 1, skip next 2 chs, **shell** *(see Special Stitches)* in last ch, turn. *(1 shell, 2 dc made)*
Row 2: Ch 4, shell in next shell, ch 1, skip next ch sp, dc in next dc, ch 2, skip next 2 chs, dc in next ch, turn.
Row 3: Ch 5 *(counts as dc and ch-2 sp)*, dc in next dc, ch 1, shell in next shell leaving ch-4 unworked, turn.
Rows 4-11: Repeat rows 2 and 3 alternately. At end of last row, **do not turn or fasten off.** *Mark last dc of last shell made.*
Row 12: For **Pineapple,** working in ends of rows, ch 3, shell in ch-4 sp at end of next row, (ch 8, skip next ch-4 sp, shell in next ch-4 sp) 2 times, turn. *(3 shells)* *Mark row 12.*
Row 13: Ch 4, shell in next shell, ch 4, skip next ch sp, 10 tr in next shell, ch 4, skip next ch sp, shell in next shell, turn. *(2 shells, 10 tr)*
Row 14: Ch 4, shell in next shell, ch 4, skip next tr, sc in next sp between tr, (ch 3, sc in next space between tr) 8 times, ch 4, shell in next shell, turn. *(2 shells, 8 ch-3 sps)*
Row 15-21: Ch 4, shell in next shell, ch 4; skipping each ch-4 sp and each sc, sc in next ch-3 sp, (ch 3, sc in next ch-3 sp) across to next ch-4 sp, ch 4, shell in next shell, turn. *(At end of last row, 2 shells, 1 ch-3 sp made.)*
Row 22: Ch 4, shell in next shell, ch 4, sc in next ch-3 sp, ch 4, 2 dc in next shell, ch 1, join with sl st in ch sp of last shell made, ch 1, 2 dc in same shell as last 2 dc made. Fasten off.

Next Section (make 5)
Row 1: With wrong side of marked row on last Section facing you, join with sl st in marked dc, repeat row 2 of First Section.
Rows 2-12: Repeat rows 3 and 2 of First Section alternately, ending with row 3.
Rows 13-23: Repeat rows 12-22 of First Section.
With tapestry needle and yarn, sew straight ends of rows on one Base to starting ch on row 1 of Center; sew other Base to last row on Center.

Edging
Join yarn with sl st in end of marked row on First Section of Border, ch 3, *(edge scallop—*see Special Stitches*—in next ch-4 sp, sc in next ch sp of shell—*beside sts already worked,* ch 3) 5 times, edge scallop in next joining sl st, ch 3, (edge scallop in next ch-4 sp, sc in next ch sp of shell, ch 3) 5 times, [sc in next ch-4 sp on Base, ch 3; working on next Pineapple, (**joined scallop**—*see Special Stitches*—in next ch-4 sp, sc in next ch sp of shell, ch 3) 3 times, (edge scallop in next ch-4 sp, sc in next ch sp of shell, ch 3) 2 times, edge scallop in next sl st, ch 3; (edge scallop in next ch-4 sp, sc in next ch sp of shell, ch 3) 5 time]; repeat between [ ] 4 more times; spacing sts evenly, dc across Base, Center and next Base*, dc in end of marked row on next Pineapple; repeat between **, join with sl st in top of ch-3. Fasten off.
On **each Border,** cut two 1-yd. pieces of ribbon. Weave through ch-2 sps on Base from edges to center of row. Fold ribbon ends under, sew to edges; tie other ends in bow at center.
Sew ribbon rose over knot.❑❑

Shawl

FINISHED SIZE:
36" x 61½".

MATERIALS:
- 13 oz. acrylic sport yarn
- F hook or hook size needed to obtain gauge

GAUGE:
3 tr, 3 chs = 1".

BASIC STITCHES:
Ch, sl st, sc, hdc, dc, tr.

SPECIAL STITCHES:
For **beginning shell, (beg shell),** sl st in next 2 sts, (sl st, ch 4, 2 tr, ch 3, 3 tr) in next ch-2 sp.

For **shell,** (3 tr, ch 2, 3 tr) in specified ch sp.

For **5-tr cluster (5-tr cl),** yo 2 times, skip next ch sp, insert hook in next ch sp, yo, pull through sp, (yo, pull through 2 lps on hook) 2 times, *yo 2 times, insert hook in next ch sp, yo, pull through sp, (yo, pull through 2 lps on hook) 2 times; repeat from * 3 more times, yo, pull through all 6 lps on hook, ch 1.

SHAWL
Row 1: Beginning at bottom, ch 5, 2 tr in fifth ch from hook, ch 2, 3 tr in same ch, turn. *(6 tr made)*
Row 2: Beg shell *(see Special Stitches)*, ch 1, **shell** *(see Special Stitches)* in same ch sp, turn. *(2 shells)*
Row 3: Beg shell, ch 4, tr in next ch-1 sp, ch 4, shell in ch sp of last shell, turn.
Row 4: Beg shell, ch 4, tr in next ch sp, ch 1, tr in next ch sp, ch 4, shell in last shell, turn.
Row 5: Beg shell, ch 4; for **pineapple,** (tr in next ch sp, ch 1) 2 times, tr in next ch sp; ch 4, shell in last shell, turn. *(2 shells, 3 tr)*
Row 6: Beg shell, ch 2, 3 tr in same shell, ch 3, (tr in next ch sp, ch 1) 3 times, tr in next ch sp, ch 3, shell in last shell, ch 2, 3 tr in same shell, turn.
Row 7: Beg shell, ch 1, shell in next ch-2 sp, ch 3, (tr in next ch sp, ch 1) 4 times, tr in next ch sp, ch 3, shell in next ch-2 sp, ch 1, shell in last ch-2 sp, turn.
Row 8: Beg shell, *ch 4, tr in next ch-1 sp, ch 4, shell in next shell*, ch 3, (tr in next ch sp, ch 1) 5 times, tr in next ch sp, ch 3, shell in next shell; repeat between **, turn. *(4 shells, 8 tr)*
Row 9: Beg shell, *ch 4, tr in next ch sp, ch 1, tr in next ch sp, ch 4, shell in next shell*, ch 3, **5-tr cl** *(see Special Stitches)*, ch 3, skip next ch sp, shell in next shell; repeat between **, turn.
Row 10: Beg shell, *ch 4, (tr in next ch sp, ch 1) 2 times, tr in next ch sp, ch 4, shell in next shell*, ch 3, sc in top of 5-tr cl, ch 3, shell in next shell; repeat between **, turn.
Row 11: Beg shell, ch 2, 3 tr in same shell, *ch 4, (tr in next ch sp, ch 1) 3 times, tr in next ch

sp, ch 4, shell in next shell*, ch 3, sc in next sc, ch 3, shell in next shell; repeat between **, ch 2, 3 tr in same shell, turn.

Row 12: Beg shell, ch 1, shell in next ch-2 sp, *ch 3, (tr in next ch sp, ch 1) 4 times, tr in next ch sp, ch 3*, shell in next ch-2 sp, ch 1, shell in next shell; repeat between **, shell in next ch-2 sp, ch 1, shell in last ch-2 sp, turn. *(6 shells, 10 tr)*

Row 13: Beg shell, *[ch 4, tr in next ch-1 sp, ch 4, shell in next shell], ch 3, (tr in next ch sp, ch 1) 5 times, tr in next ch sp, ch 3, shell in next shell; repeat from * one more time; repeat between [ ], turn.

Row 14: Beg shell, *[ch 4, tr in next ch sp, ch 1, tr in next ch sp, ch 4, shell in next shell], ch 3, 5-tr cl, ch 3, shell in next shell; repeat from * one more time; repeat between [ ], turn.

Row 15: Beg shell, *[ch 4, (tr in next ch sp, ch 1) 2 times, tr in next ch sp, ch 4, shell in next shell], ch 3, sc in top of 5-tr cl, ch 3, shell in next shell; repeat from * one more time; repeat between [ ], turn.

Row 16: Beg shell, ch 2, 3 tr in same shell, *[ch 4, (tr in next ch sp, ch 1) 3 times, tr in next ch sp, ch 4, shell in next shell], ch 3, sc in next sc, ch 3, shell in next shell; repeat from * one more time; repeat between [ ], ch 2, 3 tr in same shell, turn.

Row 17: Beg shell, ch 1, shell in next ch-2 sp, *[ch 3, (tr in next ch sp, ch 1) 4 times, tr in next ch sp, ch 3], shell in next shell, ch 1, shell in next shell; repeat from * one more time; repeat between [ ], shell in next ch-2 sp, ch 1, shell in last ch-2 sp, turn. *(8 shells, 15 tr)*

Row 18: Beg shell, *[ch 4, tr in next ch-1 sp, ch 4, shell in next shell], ch 3, (tr in next ch sp, ch 1) 5 times, tr in next ch sp, ch 3, shell in next shell; repeat from * across to last shell; repeat between [ ], turn.

Row 19: Beg shell, (*ch 4, tr in next ch sp, ch 1, tr in next ch sp, ch 4, shell in next shell*, ch 3, 5-tr cl, ch 3, shell in next shell) across to last pineapple; repeat between **, turn.

Row 20: Beg shell, *[ch 4, (tr in next ch sp, ch 1) 2 times, tr in next ch sp, ch 4, shell in next shell], ch 3, sc in top of 5-tr cl, ch 3, shell in next shell; repeat from * across to last pineapple; repeat between [ ], turn.

Row 21: Beg shell, ch 2, 3 tr in same shell, *[ch 4, (tr in next ch sp, ch 1) 3 times, tr in next ch sp, ch 4, shell in next shell], ch 3, sc in next sc, ch 3, shell in next shell; repeat from * across to last pineapple; repeat between [ ], ch 2, 3 tr in same shell, turn.

Row 22: Beg shell, ch 1, shell in next ch-2 sp, *[ch 3, (tr in next ch sp, ch 1) 4 times, tr in next ch sp, ch 3], shell in next shell, ch 1, shell in next shell; repeat from * across to last pineapple; repeat between [ ], shell in next ch-2 sp, ch 1, shell in last ch-2 sp, turn.

Rows 23-49: Or to desired length, repeat rows 18-22 consecutively, ending with row 19.

Row 50: Ch 1, sc in first 3 sts, *(sc in next ch sp, sc in next 3 sts, 3 sc in next ch sp, sc in next st, sc in next ch sp, sc in next st, 3 sc in next ch sp, sc in next 3 sts, sc in next ch sp*, hdc in next st, dc in next st, tr in next st, ch 1, skip next 2 ch sps, tr in next st, dc in next st, hdc in next st) across to last pineapple; repeat between **, sc in last 3 sts, turn.

Row 51: (Ch 4, 2 tr) in first st, skip next 2 sts, *(sc, ch 4, 2 tr) in next st, skip next 3 sts or ch; repeat from * across to last 4 sts, (sc, ch 4, 2 tr) in next st, skip next 2 sts, sc in last st. Fasten off.

For **each fringe,** cut three strands each 17" long. With all three strands held together, fold in half, insert hook in ch-2 sp of shell at end of row, pull fold through sp, pull ends through fold, tighten. Fringe in ch-2 sp at end of each row, bottom of row 1 and in each corner.❑❑

Pillowcase Edging

FINISHED SIZE:
Fits standard-size pillowcase.

MATERIALS:
- ❑ 440 yds. size 10 crochet cotton thread
- ❑ ⅔ yd. ⅝" ribbon
- ❑ Sewing thread to match ribbon
- ❑ Sewing and tapestry needles
- ❑ No. 10 steel hook or hook size needed to obtain gauge

GAUGE:
11 sts = 1"; dc = ¼".

BASIC STITCHES:
Ch, sl st, sc, dc.

SPECIAL STITCH:
For **shell,** (2 dc, ch 2, 2 dc) in specified st.

EDGING

Row 1: Ch 55, sc in eighth ch from hook, (ch 5, skip next 3 chs, dc in next ch) 2 times, ch 7, skip next 4 chs, dc in next ch, (ch 5, skip next 3 chs, sc in next ch) 5 times, (ch 5, skip next 4 chs, sc in next ch) 2 times, ch 5, skip next 3 chs, **shell** *(see Special Stitch)* in last ch, turn. *(12 ch sps, 1 shell made)*

Row 2: Ch 7, shell in ch sp of first shell, ch 5, skip next ch sp, dc in next ch sp, ch 7, dc in next ch sp, ch 5, skip next ch sp, shell in next ch sp, ch 5, (sc in next ch sp, ch 5) 3 times, 10 sc in next ch sp, (ch 5, sc in next ch sp) 3 times, turn. *(10 ch sps, 10 sc, 2 shells) Front of row 2 is right side of work.*

Row 3: Ch 7, sc in first ch sp, ch 5, sc in next ch sp, ch 5, dc in next ch sp, ch 7, dc in next ch sp, ch 5, (sc in next ch sp, ch 5) 3 times, shell in next shell, ch 5, skip next ch sp, 17 dc in next ch sp, ch 5, shell in last shell, turn. *(17 dc, 10 ch sps, 10 sc, 2 shells)*

Row 4: Ch 7, shell in first shell, ch 5, skip next ch sp and next dc, sc in **back lps** *(see Stitch Guide)* of next 15 dc, ch 5, skip next dc

and next ch sp, shell in next shell, ch 5, (sc in next ch sp, ch 5) 4 times, 10 sc in next ch sp, (ch 5, sc in next ch sp) 3 times, turn.

Row 5: Ch 7, sc in first ch sp, ch 5, sc in next ch sp, ch 5, dc in next ch sp, ch 7, dc in next ch sp, ch 5, (sc in next ch sp, ch 5) 4 times, shell in next shell, ch 5, skip next ch sp and next sc, sc in next sc, (ch 2, sc in next sc) 13 times, ch 5, shell in last shell, turn.

Row 6: Ch 7, shell in first shell, ch 5, skip next 2 ch sps, sc in next ch sp, (ch 2, sc in next ch sp) 11 times, ch 5, shell in next shell, ch 5, (sc in next ch sp, ch 5) 5 times, 10 sc in next ch sp, (ch 5, sc in next ch sp) 3 times, turn.

Row 7: Ch 7, sc in first ch sp, ch 5, sc in next ch sp, ch 5, dc in next ch sp, ch 7, dc in next ch sp, ch 5, (sc in next ch sp, ch 5) 5 times, shell in next shell, ch 5, skip next 2 ch sps, sc in next ch sp, (ch 2, sc in next ch sp) 9 times,

ch 5, shell in last shell, turn.

Row 8: Ch 7, shell in first shell, ch 5, skip next 2 ch sps, sc in next ch sp, (ch 2, sc in next ch sp) 7 times, ch 5, shell in next shell, ch 5, (sc in next ch sp, ch 5) 6 times, 10 sc in next ch sp, (ch 5, sc in next ch sp) 3 times, turn.

Row 9: Ch 7, sc in first ch sp, ch 5, sc in next ch sp, ch 5, dc in next ch sp, ch 7, dc in next ch sp, ch 5, (sc in next ch sp, ch 5) 6 times, shell in next shell, ch 5, skip next 2 ch sps, sc in next ch sp, (ch 2, sc in next ch sp) 5 times, ch 5, shell in last shell, turn.

Row 10: Ch 7, shell in first shell, ch 5, skip next 2 ch sps, sc in next ch sp, (ch 2, sc in next ch sp) 3 times, ch 5, shell in next shell, ch 5, (sc in next ch sp, ch 5) 7 times, 10 sc in next ch sp, (ch 5, sc in next ch sp) 3 times, turn.

Row 11: Ch 7, sc in first ch sp, ch 5, sc in next ch sp, ch 5, dc in next ch sp, ch 7, dc in next ch sp, ch 5, (sc in next ch sp, ch 5) 7 times, shell in next shell, ch 5, skip next 2 ch sps, sc in next ch sp, ch 5, shell in last shell, turn.

Row 12: Ch 7, shell in first shell, shell in next shell, ch 5, (sc in next ch sp, ch 5) 8 times, 10 sc in next ch sp, (ch 5, sc in next ch sp) 3 times, turn.

Row 13: Ch 7, sc in first ch sp, ch 5, sc in next ch sp, ch 5, dc in next ch sp, ch 7, dc in next ch sp, ch 5, (sc in next ch sp, ch 5) 7 times, shell in next shell, sc in next shell, turn, completing pattern.

Repeat rows 2-13 and continue pattern 13 more times or until piece measures 44". At end of last row, fasten off.

Sew first and last rows together. With right side facing you, work 10 sc over seam in same man-ner as other rows. Fasten off.

Starting at seam, join with sc in end of last row, sc in same row, 11 sc in next ch-7 sp, (2 sc in end of next row, 11 sc in next ch-7 sp) around, join with sl st in first sc. Fasten off.

Weave ribbon through 10-sc sps. Sew ends together.

Sew over hem of pillowcase as desired.❑❑

Pineapple Motif Tablecloth

FINISHED SIZE:
Each Motif measures 5½" square before blocking. A tablecloth 12 Motifs x 16 Motifs is 68" x 90".

MATERIALS:
- ❑ 12,040 yds. size 10 crochet cotton thread
- ❑ No. 10 steel hook or hook size needed to obtain gauge

GAUGE:
10 sts = 1"; dc = ¼" tall.

BASIC STITCHES:
Ch, sl st, sc, dc, tr.

SPECIAL STITCHES:
For **beginning cluster (beg cl),** ch 4, *yo 2 times, insert hook in ring or st, yo, pull lp through, (yo, pull through 2 lps on hook) 2 times; repeat from * one more time, yo, pull through all 3 lps on hook.

For **cluster (cl),** *yo 2 times, insert hook in ring or ch sp, yo, pull lp through, (yo, pull through 2 lps on hook) 2 times; repeat from * 2 more times, yo, pull through all 4 lps on hook.

For **6-double crochet decrease (6-dc dec),** (yo, insert hook in next st, yo, pull through st, yo, pull through 2 lps on hook) 6 times, yo, pull through all 7 lps on hook.

FIRST MOTIF
Rnd 1: Starting at center, ch 10, sl st in first ch to form ring, **beg cl** *(see Special Stitches),* ch 4, (**cl**— *see Special Stitches,* ch 4) 7 times, join with sl st in top of beg cl. *(8 cls, 8 ch sps made)*
Rnd 2: (Sl st, ch 4, 2 tr) in first ch sp, ch 4, 5 tr in next ch sp, ch 4,

(3 tr in next ch sp, ch 4, 5 tr in next ch sp, ch 4) around, join with sl st in top of first ch-4. *(32 tr)*

Rnd 3: (Ch 3, dc) in first sl st, *(dc, ch 2, dc) in next tr, 2 dc in next tr, ch 4, sc in next 5 tr, ch 4*, (2 dc in next tr; repeat between **) around, join with sl st in top of ch-3.

Rnd 4: Ch 3, dc in next 2 dc, *(dc, ch 2, dc) in next ch sp, dc in next 3 dc, (ch 4, sc in next sc) 5 times, ch 4*, (dc in next 3 dc; repeat between **) around, join.

Rnd 5: Ch 3, dc in next 2 dc, *ch 2, skip next dc, (dc, ch 2) 4 times in next ch sp, skip next dc, dc in next 3 dc, (ch 4, skip next sc, sc in next ch sp) 4 times, ch 4*, (dc in next 3 dc; repeat between **) around, join.

Rnd 6: Ch 3, dc in next 2 dc, *(ch 2, dc in next ch sp) 3 times, ch 2, dc in same ch sp, (ch 2, dc in next ch sp) 2 times, ch 2, dc in next 3 dc, (ch 4, skip next sc, sc in next ch sp) 3 times, ch 4*, (dc in next 3 dc; repeat between **) around, join.

Rnd 7: Ch 3, dc in next 2 dc, *(ch 2, dc in next ch sp) 3 times, ch 2, 4 dc in next ch sp, (ch 2, dc in next ch sp) 3 times, ch 2, dc in next 3 dc, (ch 4, skip next sc, sc in next ch sp) 2 times, ch 4*, (dc in next 3 dc; repeat between **) around, join.

Rnd 8: Ch 3, dc in next 2 dc, *(ch 2, dc in next ch sp) 3 times, ch 2, 4 dc in next ch sp, ch 3, 4 dc in next ch sp, (ch 2, dc in next ch sp) 3 times, ch 2, dc in next 3 dc, ch 4, skip next sc, sc in next ch sp, ch 4*, (dc in next 3 dc; repeat between **) around, join.

Rnd 9: Ch 3, dc in next 2 dc, *(ch 2, dc in next ch sp) 4 times, (ch 2, cl) 4 times in next ch sp, (ch 2, dc in next ch sp) 4 times, ch 2, dc in next 3 dc, skip next ch-4 sp, skip next sc, skip next ch-4 sp*, (dc in next 3 dc; repeat between **) around, join.

Rnd 10: Sl st in next 2 dc, sl st in next ch-2 sp, sl st in next dc, ch 3, *2 dc in next ch sp, dc in next dc, ch 2, dc in next dc, 2 dc in next ch sp, dc in next dc, ch 2, dc in tip of next cl, ch 2, skip next ch sp, skip next cl, (tr, ch 2) 5 times in next ch sp, skip next cl, skip next ch sp, dc in tip of next cl, (ch 2, dc in next dc, 2 dc in next ch sp, dc in next dc) 2 times, ch 4, skip next ch sp, **6-dc dec** *(see Special Stitches)*, ch 4, skip next ch sp*, (dc in next dc; repeat between **) around, join. Fasten off.

SECOND MOTIF
Rnds 1-9: Repeat rnds 1-9 of First Motif.

Rnd 10: Sl st in next 2 dc, sl st in the next ch-2 sp, sl st in next dc, ch 3, 2 dc in next ch sp, dc in next dc, ch 2, dc in next dc, 2 dc in next ch sp, dc in next dc, ch 2, dc in tip of next cl, ch 2, skip next ch sp, skip next cl, (tr, ch 2, tr, ch 2, tr) in next ch sp, (ch 1, sc in corresponding ch sp on First Motif, ch 1, tr in same corner ch sp on Motif in work) 2 times, ch 1, sc in corresponding ch sp on First Motif, ch 1, skip next cl, skip next ch sp on Motif in work, dc in tip of next cl, (ch 1, sc in corresponding ch sp on First Motif, ch 1, dc in next dc on Motif in work, 2 dc in next ch sp, dc in next dc) 2 times, ch 2, sc in corresponding ch sp on First Motif, ch 2, 6-dc dec on Motif in work; this completes half of joining, join other half to correspond and complete remainder of rnd as for First Motif.

Make 12 rows of 16 Motifs, joining them in same manner as Second Motif was joined to First *(corner tr's are not joined)*; Motifs joined on two sides are worked in same manner as Second Motif repeating first joining on second joined side.

EDGING
Rnd 1: Join with sl st in center tr at 1 corner of tablecloth, ch 8, dc in same st as sl st, *(ch 2, dc in next ch sp) 4 times, (ch 2, skip next 2 dc, dc in next dc, ch 2, dc in next ch sp) 2 times, ch 2, dc in tip of next dec, ch 2, dc in next ch sp, (ch 2, skip next 2 dc, dc in next dc, ch 2, dc in next ch sp) 2 times, (ch 2, dc in next ch sp) 3 times, ch 2, dc in next tr, ch 2, dc in center tr at corner of next Motif; repeat from * around, making (dc, ch 5, dc) in center tr at each corner, join with sl st in third ch of beginning ch-8.

Rnd 2: Sl st in first ch sp, beg cl, (ch 5, cl in same ch sp as last cl) 2 times, (ch 5, skip next ch sp, cl in next ch sp) around, making (cl, ch 5, cl, ch 5, cl) in ch sp at each corner, join with sl st in tip of beg cl.

Rnd 3: (Sl st, ch 5, dc) in next ch sp, ch 2, (dc, ch 5, dc) in tip of next cl, *ch 2, (dc, ch 2, dc) in next ch sp; repeat from * around, making (dc, ch 5, dc) in each corner, join.

Rnd 4: (Sl st, sc) in first ch sp, *ch 5, skip next ch sp, (dc, ch 3, dc) in next corner ch sp, ch 5, skip next ch sp, sc in next ch sp; repeat from * around, always having (dc, ch 3, dc) in each corner ch sp, join with sl st in first sc. Fasten off. ❑❑

Pineapple Afghan

Designed by Judy Teague Treece

FINISHED SIZE:
58" x 77".

MATERIALS:
- ❑ 48 oz. worsted yarn
- ❑ J hook or hook size needed to obtain gauge

GAUGE:
5 dc = 2"; 5 dc rnds = 2"; rnds 1-2 = 3½" across. Each Square is 18½".

BASIC STITCHES:
Ch, sl st, sc, dc.

AFGHAN
Square (make 12)
Row 1: Ch 5, sl st in first ch to form ring, ch 2, (yo, insert hook in ring, yo, pull lp through, yo, pull through 2 lps on hook) 2 times, yo, pull through all lps on hook *(beg cluster made)*, ch 2; *for **cluster**, (yo, insert hook in ring, yo, pull lp through, yo, pull

through 2 lps on hook) 3 times, yo, pull through all lps on hook, ch 2; repeat from * 6 more times, join with sl st in top of beg cluster. *(8 clusters, 8 ch sps made)*

Row 2: (Sl st, ch 3, 2 dc, ch 2, 3 dc) in first ch-2 sp, ch 1, 3 dc in next ch-2 sp, ch 1, *(3 dc, ch 2, 3 dc) in next ch-2 sp, ch 1, 3 dc in next ch-2 sp, ch 1; repeat from * 2 more times, join with sl st in top of ch-3.

Row 3: Sl st in next 2 sts, (sc, ch 5,

sc) in first ch-2 sp, ch 3, skip next 3 dc, next ch-1 and next dc, (dc, ch 2, dc) in next dc, ch 3, skip next dc, next ch-1 and next 3 dc, *(sc, ch 5, sc) in next ch-2 sp, ch 3, skip next 3 dc, next ch-1 and next dc, (dc, ch 2, dc) in next dc, ch 3, skip next dc, next ch-1 and next 3 dc; repeat from * 2 more times, join with sl st in first sc.

Note: Do not join following rnds unless otherwise stated. Mark first st of each rnd.

Rnd 4: Working in continuous rnds, sc in first ch-5 sp, ch 2 *(sc and ch-2 count as first dc)*, 8 dc in same ch-5 sp as first sc, ch 2, skip next ch-3 sp, dc in next dc, (dc, ch 2, dc) in next ch-2 sp, dc in next dc, ch 2, skip next ch-3 sp, *9 dc in next ch-5 sp, ch 2, skip next ch-3 sp, dc in next dc, (dc, ch 2, dc) in next ch-2 sp, dc in next dc, ch 2, skip next ch-3 sp; repeat from * 2 more times.

Rnd 5: *(Sc in next dc, ch 1) 8 times, sc in next dc, ch 2, skip next ch-2 sp, dc in next 2 dc, (dc, ch 2, dc) in next ch-2 sp, dc in next 2 dc, ch 2, skip next ch-2 sp; repeat from * around.

Rnd 6: *(Sc in next ch-1 sp, ch 1) 7 times, sc in next ch-1 sp, ch 2, skip next ch-2 sp, dc in next 3 dc, (dc, ch 2, dc) in next ch-2 sp, dc in next 3 dc, ch 2, skip next ch-2 sp; repeat from * around.

Rnd 7: *(Sc in next ch-1 sp, ch 1) 6 times, sc in next ch-1 sp, ch 2, skip next ch-2 sp, dc in next 4 dc, (dc, ch 2, dc) in next ch-2 sp, dc in next 4 dc, ch 2, skip next ch-2 sp; repeat from * around.

Rnd 8: *(Sc in next ch-1 sp, ch 1) 5 times, sc in next ch-1 sp, ch 2, skip next ch-2 sp, dc in next 5 dc, (dc, ch 2, dc) in next ch-2 sp, dc in next 5 dc, ch 2, skip next ch-2 sp; repeat from * around.

Rnd 9: *(Sc in next ch-1 sp, ch 1) 4 times, sc in next ch-1 sp, ch 2, skip next ch-2 sp, dc in next 6 dc, (dc, ch 2, dc) in next ch-2 sp, dc in next 6 dc, ch 2, skip next ch-2 sp; repeat from * around.

Rnd 10: *(Sc in next ch-1 sp, ch 1) 3 times, sc in next ch-1 sp, ch 3, skip next ch-2 sp, dc in next 7 dc, (dc, ch 2, dc) in next ch-2 sp, dc in next 7 dc, ch 3, skip next ch-2 sp; repeat from * around.

Rnd 11: *(Sc in next ch-1 sp, ch 1) 2 times, sc in next ch-1 sp, ch 3, skip next ch-3 sp, dc in next 8 dc, (dc, ch 2, dc) in next ch-2 sp, dc in next 8 dc, ch 3, skip next ch-3 sp; repeat from * around.

Rnd 12: *[Sc in next ch-1 sp, ch 1, sc in next ch-1 sp, ch 3, skip next ch-3 sp, dc in next 9 dc, (dc, ch 2, dc) in next ch-2 sp, dc in next 9 dc], ch 3, skip next ch-3 sp; repeat from * 2 more times; repeat between [-], ch 5, skip last ch-3 sp.

Rnd 13: *[Sc in next ch-1 sp, ch 5, dc in next 10 dc, (dc, ch 2, dc) in next ch-2 sp, dc in next 10 dc], ch 5, skip next ch-3 sp; repeat from * 2 more times; repeat between [-].

Rnd 14: *[Ch 4, sc in next ch-5 sp, ch 3, sc in next ch-5 sp, ch 4, dc in next 11 dc, (dc, ch 2, dc) in next ch-2 sp, dc in next 11 dc]; repeat from * 2 more times; repeat between [-].

Rnd 15: *[Ch 3, skip next ch-4 sp, (dc, ch 2, dc) in next ch-3 sp, ch 3, skip next ch-4 sp, dc in next 12 dc, (dc, ch 2, dc) in next ch-2 sp, dc in next 12 dc]; repeat from * 2 more times; repeat between [-].

Rnd 16: *[4 dc in next ch-3 sp, 2 dc in next ch-2 sp, 4 dc in next ch-3 sp, dc in next 13 dc, (dc, ch 2, dc) in next ch-2 sp, dc in next 13 dc]; repeat from * 2 more times; repeat between [-].

Rnd 17: Sc in each dc around with (sc, ch 1, sc) in each ch-2 sp, join with sl st in first sc. Fasten off. Block if desired.

ASSEMBLY

For seam, hold two Squares with right sides together, matching sts and corner ch sps; working in **back lps** *(see Stitch Guide)* of both Squares, join with sl st in corner ch sp, sl st loosely in each st across to next corner ch sp, sl st in corner ch sp. Fasten off.

Repeat with remaining Squares, forming a piece three Squares wide and four Squares long.

BORDER

Rnd 1: Working around outer edge, join with sc in st before first corner ch-1 sp on one short end, 3 sc in corner ch-1 sp, sc in each st and in each seam around with 3 sc in each corner ch-1 sp, join with sl st in first sc. *(582 sc)*

Rnd 2: Ch 1, sc in first st, [ch 3, skip next st, (dc, ch 1) 4 times in next st, dc in same st as last dc made *(corner made)*, ch 3, skip next st, sc in next st, *ch 3, skip next 2 sts, (dc, ch 1) 4 times in next st, dc in same st as last dc made, ch 3, skip next 2 sts, sc in next st*; repeat between ** 19 more times, ch 3, skip next 2 sts, (dc, ch 1) 4 times in next st, dc in same st as last dc made, ch 3, skip next st, sc in next st]; repeat between ** 27 times; repeat between [-]; repeat between ** 26 times, ch 3, skip next 2 sts, (dc, ch 1) 4 times in next st, dc in same st as last dc made, ch 3, skip last 2 sts, join with sl st in first sc. Fasten off.❏❏

Table Runner

An Original by Annie

FINISHED SIZE:
18" x 68".

MATERIALS:
- ❑ 2,000 yds. size 10 crochet cotton thread
- ❑ No. 4 steel hook or hook needed to obtain gauge

GAUGE:
1 shell = ½"; 3 shell rows = 1".

BASIC STITCHES:
Ch, sl st, sc, dc, tr.

SPECIAL STITCH:
For **shell,** (3 dc, ch 2, 3 dc) in ch sp of next shell.

RUNNER
Foundation
(Ch 4, tr in fourth ch from hook) 31 times, turn. *(31 ch sps made)*

First Side
Row 1: Working in ch-3 sps at ends of rows across one side of Foundation, (sl st, ch 3, 2 dc, ch 2, 3 dc) in first ch sp, (ch 8, skip next 2 ch sps, **shell**—*see Special Stitch*— in next ch sp) across, turn. *(11 shells, 10 ch-8 sps made)*

Row 2: Ch 3, shell, (ch 5, 12 tr in ch sp of next shell, ch 5, shell) across, turn.

Row 3: Ch 3, shell, *ch 3, (dc in next tr, ch 1) 11 times, dc in next tr, ch 3, shell; repeat from * across, turn.

Row 4: Ch 3, shell, *ch 3, skip next ch sp, (sc in next ch-1 sp, ch 3) 11 times, shell; repeat from * across, turn.

Row 5: Ch 3, shell, *ch 3, skip next ch sp, (sc in next ch sp, ch 3) 10 times, shell; repeat from * across, turn.

Row 6: Ch 3, shell, *ch 3, skip next ch sp, (sc in next ch sp, ch 3) 9 times, shell; repeat from * across, turn.

Row 7: Ch 3, shell, *ch 3, skip

next ch sp, (sc in next ch sp, ch 3) 8 times, (3 dc, ch 2, 3 dc, ch 2, 3 dc) in next ch sp; repeat from * 3 more times, ch 3, skip next ch sp, (sc in next ch sp, ch 3) 8 times, shell, turn.

Row 8: Ch 3, shell, *skip next ch sp, (sc in next ch sp, ch 3) 7 times, (shell in next ch-2 sp, ch 2) 2 times; repeat from * 3 more times, ch 3, skip next ch sp, (sc in next ch sp, ch 3) 7 times, shell, turn.

Row 9: Ch 3, shell, *ch 3, skip next ch sp, (sc in next ch sp, ch 3) 6 times, shell, ch 2, shell in next ch-2 sp, ch 2, shell; repeat from * 3 more times, ch 3, skip next ch sp, (sc in next ch sp, ch 3) 6 times, shell, turn.

Row 10: Ch 3, shell, *ch 3, skip next ch sp, (sc in next ch sp, ch 3) 5 times, (shell, ch 3) 2 times, shell; repeat from * 3 more times, ch 3, skip next ch sp, (sc in next ch sp, ch 3) 5 times, shell, turn.

Row 11: Ch 3, shell, *ch 3, skip next ch sp, (sc in next ch sp, ch 3) 4 times, (shell, ch 5) 2 times, shell; repeat from * 3 more times, ch 3, skip next ch sp, (sc in next ch sp, ch 3) 4 times, shell, turn.

Row 12: Ch 3, shell, *ch 3, skip next ch sp, (sc in next ch sp, ch 3) 3 times, shell, ch 3, 12 tr in ch sp of next shell, ch 3, shell; repeat from * 3 more times, ch 3, skip next ch sp, (sc in next ch sp, ch 3) 3 times, shell, turn.

Row 13: Ch 3, shell, *ch 3, skip next ch sp, (sc in next ch sp, ch 3) 2 times, shell, ch 3, (dc in next tr, ch 1) 11 times, dc in next tr, ch 3, shell; repeat from * 3 more times, ch 3, skip next ch sp, (sc in next ch sp, ch 3) 2 times, shell, turn.

Row 14: Ch 3, *shell, ch 3, skip next ch sp, sc in next ch sp, ch 3, shell, ch 3, skip next ch sp, (sc in next ch sp, ch 3) 11 times; repeat from * 3 more times, shell, ch 3, skip next ch sp, sc in next ch sp, ch 3, shell, turn.

Row 15: Ch 3, shell, ch 2, shell, *ch 3, skip next ch sp, (sc in next ch sp, ch 3) 10 times, shell, ch 2, shell; repeat from * across, turn.

Row 16: Ch 3, (shell, ch 2) 2 times, shell, *ch 3, skip next ch sp, (sc in next ch sp, ch 3) 9 times, (shell, ch 2) 2 times, shell; repeat from * across, turn.

Row 17: Ch 3, (shell, ch 3) 2 times, shell, *ch 3, skip next ch sp, (sc in next ch sp, ch 3) 8 times, (shell, ch 3) 2 times, shell; repeat from * across, turn.

Row 18: Ch 3, *(shell, ch 3) 3 times, skip next ch sp, (sc in next ch sp, ch 3) 7 times; repeat from * across to last 3 shells, (shell, ch 3) 2 times, shell, turn.

Row 19: Ch 3, shell, ch 3, 12 tr in ch sp of next shell, *ch 3, shell, ch 3, skip next ch sp, (sc in next

ch sp, ch 3) 6 times, shell, ch 3, 12 tr in ch sp of next shell, ch 3, shell; repeat from * across, turn.

Row 20: Ch 3, shell, ch 3, (dc in next tr, ch 1) 11 times, dc in next tr, ch 3, *shell, ch 3, skip next ch sp, (sc in next ch sp, ch 3) 5 times, shell, ch 3, (dc in next tr, ch 1) 11 times, dc in next tr, ch 3; repeat from * across, shell, turn.

Row 21: Ch 3, shell, ch 3, (sc in next ch-1 sp, ch 3) 11 times, *shell, ch 3, skip next ch sp, (sc in next ch sp, ch 3) 4 times, shell, ch 3, (sc in next ch-1 sp, ch 3) 11 times; repeat from * across, shell, turn.

Row 22: Ch 3, shell, ch 3, skip next ch sp, (sc in next ch sp, ch 3) 10 times, *shell, ch 3, skip next ch sp, (sc in next ch sp, ch 3) 3 times, shell, ch 3, skip next ch sp, (sc in next ch sp, ch 3) 10 times; repeat from * across, shell, turn.

Row 23: Ch 3, shell, ch 3, skip next ch sp, (sc in next ch sp, ch 3) 9 times, *shell, ch 3, skip next ch sp, (sc in next ch sp, ch 3) 2 times, shell, ch 3, skip next ch sp, (sc in next ch sp, ch 3) 9 times; repeat from * across, shell, turn.

Row 24: Ch 3, shell, ch 3, skip next ch sp, (sc in next ch sp, ch 3) 8 times, *shell, ch 3, skip next ch sp, sc in next ch sp, ch 3, shell, ch 3, (sc in next ch sp, ch 3) 8 times; repeat from * across, shell, turn.

Row 25: Ch 3, shell, ch 3, skip next ch sp, (sc in next ch sp, ch 3) 7 times, *shell, ch 2, shell, ch 3, skip next ch sp, (sc in next ch sp, ch 3) 7 times; repeat from * across, shell, turn.

Row 26: Ch 3, shell, ch 3, skip next ch sp, (sc in next ch sp, ch 3) 6 times, *shell, ch 2, shell in next ch-2 sp, ch 2, shell, ch 3, skip next ch sp, (sc in next ch sp, ch 3) 6 times; repeat from * across, shell, turn.

Row 27: Ch 3, shell, ch 3, skip next ch sp, (sc in next ch sp, ch 3) 5 times, *(shell, ch 3) 3 times, skip next ch sp, (sc in next ch sp, ch 3) 5 times; repeat from * across, shell, turn.

Row 28: Ch 3, shell, ch 3, skip

next ch sp, (sc in next ch sp, ch 3) 4 times, *(shell, ch 3) 3 times, skip next ch sp, (sc in next ch sp, ch 3) 4 times; repeat from * across, shell, turn.

Rows 29–96: Repeat rows 12–28 consecutively four times.

Rows 97–110: Repeat rows 12–26. At end of last row, **do not fasten off.**

First Pineapple Point

Row 1: Ch 3, shell, ch 3, skip next ch sp, (sc in next ch sp, ch 3) 6 times, shell leaving remaining shells and ch sps unworked, turn.

Row 2: Ch 3, shell, ch 3, skip next ch sp, (sc in next ch sp, ch 3) 5 times, shell, turn.

Row 3: Ch 3, shell, ch 3, skip next ch sp, (sc in next ch sp, ch 3) 4 times, shell, turn.

Row 4: Ch 3, shell, ch 3, skip next ch sp, (sc in next ch sp, ch 3) 3 times, shell, turn.

Row 5: Ch 3, shell, ch 3, skip next ch sp, (sc in next ch sp, ch 3) 2 times, shell, turn.

Row 6: Ch 3, shell, ch 3, skip next ch sp, sc in next ch sp, ch 3, shell, turn.

Row 7: Ch 3, shell, ch 2, shell. Fasten off.

Second Pineapple Point

Row 1: Join with sl st in ch sp of next unworked shell on row 110, (ch 3, 2 dc, ch 2, 3 dc) in same ch sp, ch 3, skip next ch sp, (sc in next ch sp, ch 3) 6 times, shell leaving remaining shells and ch sps unworked, turn.

Row 2: Ch 3, shell, ch 3, skip next ch sp, (sc in next ch sp, ch 3) 5 times, shell, turn.

Row 3: Ch 3, shell, ch 3, skip next ch sp, (sc in next ch sp, ch 3) 4 times, shell, turn.

Row 4: Ch 3, shell, ch 3, skip next ch sp, (sc in next ch sp, ch 3) 3 times, shell, turn.

Row 5: Ch 3, shell, ch 3, skip next ch sp, (sc in next ch sp, ch 3) 2 times, shell, turn.

Row 6: Ch 3, shell, ch 3, skip next ch sp, sc in next ch sp, ch 3, shell, turn.

Row 7: Ch 3, shell, ch 2, shell. Fasten off.
For remaining pineapple points, repeat Second Pineapple Point 3 times.

Second Side
Row 1: Working in sps on opposite side of Foundation, join with sl st in first ch sp, (ch 3, 2 dc, ch 2, 3 dc) in first ch sp, (ch 8, skip next 2 ch sps, shell in next ch sp) across, turn. *(11 shells, 10 ch-8 sps made)*
Work remainder same as First Side and Pineapple Points. ❑❑

Pretty Pineapples

Designed by Dorris Brooks

FINISHED SIZE:
45" x 64".

MATERIALS:
❑ Worsted yarn:
  20 oz. rose pink
  9 oz. lt. pink
❑ 1 hook or hook size needed to obtain gauge

GAUGE:
3 dc = 1"; 3 pattern rows = 2".

BASIC STITCHES:
Ch, sl st, sc, dc, tr.

PANEL (make 5)
Row 1: With rose, ch 19, dc in fourth ch from hook, dc in next 5 chs, ch 3, skip next 3 chs, dc in last 7 chs, turn. *(14 dc made)*
Row 2: Ch 3, dc in next st, ch 3, 8 dc in ch-3 sp, ch 3, dc in last 2 sts, turn. *(12)*
Row 3: Ch 3, dc in next st, dc in next ch-3 sp, ch 2, dc in next 8 sts, ch 2, dc in ch-3 sp, dc in last 2 sts, turn.
Row 4: Ch 3, dc in next 2 sts, dc in ch-2 sp, ch 2, skip next st, dc in next 6 sts, ch 2, skip next st, dc in ch-2 sp, dc in last 3 sts, turn.
Row 5: Ch 3, dc in next 3 sts, dc in ch-2 sp, ch 2, skip next st, dc in next 4 sts, ch 2, skip next st, dc in ch-2 sp, dc in last 4 sts, turn.
Row 6: Ch 3, dc in next 4 sts, dc in ch-2 sp, ch 2, skip next st, dc in next 2 sts, ch 2, skip next st, dc in next ch sp, dc in last 5 sts, turn.
Row 7: Ch 3, dc in next 5 sts, dc in ch-2 sp, ch 3, skip next 2 sts, dc in ch-2 sp, dc in last 6 sts, turn.
Rows 8-85: Repeat rows 2-7 consecutively. At end of last row, fasten off.

BORDER

Rnd 1: Working in ends of rows, with right side facing you, join rose with sl st in end of last row, ch 3, (dc, ch 2, 2 dc) in end of same row, dc in end or next row; for ***V-st, (dc, ch 1, dc)** in end of next row, dc in end of next row; repeat from *across to last row, (2 dc, ch 2, 2 dc) in end of last row; working in remaining lps on opposite side of starting ch , ch 3, skip next 2 sts, sc in next st, (3 dc, tr, ch 3, tr, 3 dc) in ch-3 sp, skip next 3 sts, sc in next st, ch 3; working in ends of rows, (2 dc, ch 2, 2 dc) in end of next row, dc in end of next row, (V-st in end of next row, dc in end of next row) across to end of last row, (2 dc, ch 2, 2 dc) in end of last row; working in sts, ch 3, skip next 2 sts, sc in next st, (3 dc, tr, ch 3, tr, 3 dc) in next ch-3 sp, skip next 3 sts,

sc in next st, ch 3, join with sl st in first dc. Fasten off.

Rnd 2: Join lt. pink with dc in first V-st, ch 1, dc in same st, **dc fp** *(see Stitch Guide)* around next st, (V-st in next V-st, dc fp around next st) across to 2 sts before corner ch sp, *skip next st, V-st in next st, (dc, ch 1) 3 times in ch-2 sp, dc in same ch sp, V-st in next st, skip next st, sc in next ch-3 sp, skip next 2 sts, (dc, in next st, ch 1) 3 times, (dc, ch 1) 4 times in next ch-2 sp, (dc in next st, ch 1) 2 times dc in next st, sc in next ch-3 sp, skip next st, V-st in next st (dc, ch 1), 3 times in next ch-2 sp, dc in same sp, V-st in next st, skip next st, dc fp around next st*, (V-st in next V-st, dc fp around next st) across to 2 sts before next corner ch-2 sp; repeat **, join. Fasten off.

Rnd 3: Join rose with sc in first dc fp, *sc in each st and in each ch

sp across to corner 4-dc group, (sc in next st, ch 1) 3 times, sc in next 2 sts, sc in next ch-1 sp, sc in next st, skip next sc, (sc in next st, ch 1) 9 times, sc in next st, skip next sc, sc in next st, sc in next ch-1 sp, sc in next 2 sts, (ch 1, sc in next st) 3 times, sc in next st; repeat from * one time, sc in each st and in each ch sp across, join with sl st in first sc. Fasten off.

ASSEMBLY

With wrong sides together, working from first V-st to last V-st on one long side, join rose with sc in first V-st on first Panel, ch 1, sl st in first V-st on second Panel, (ch 1, skip next st on first Panel, sl st in next st, ch 1, skip next st, sl st in corresponding st on second Panel) across. Fasten off. Repeat until all Panels are joined.❏❏

Tissue Cover

An Original by Annie

FINISHED SIZE:
Fits boutique-size tissue box.

MATERIALS:
❏ For Cover, 3½ oz. acrylic sport yarn or 450 yds. size 10 crochet cotton thread
❏ For Pineapple Lace, 230 yds. size 10 crochet cotton thread
❏ ½ yd. of ¼" ribbon
❏ Tapestry needle
❏ No. 0 and No. 7 steel hooks or hook size needed to obtain gauge

GAUGE:
No. 0 steel hook and one strand acrylic sport yarn or two strands crochet cotton, 13 sc = 2"; 7 sc **back lp rows** = 1".

BASIC STITCHES:
Ch, sl st, sc, hdc, dc, tr.

COVER
Notes: *For acrylic sport yarn, use*

single strand; for size 10 crochet cotton thread, use two strands held together.

Place piece on tissue box as you work to check fit of Cover.

Row 1: With No. 0 hook and yarn, ch 49, sc in second ch from hook, sc in each ch across, turn. *(48 sc made)*

Rows 2-128: Working in **back lps** *(see Stitch Guide)*, ch 1, sc in each st across, turn.

Row 129: Hold ends together and sl st bottom edge of first row and back lps of last row together. Turn seam to inside so it will not show. **Do not fasten off.**

Top Opening

Ch 3, (skip end of next row, work first half of a dc in end of next row, skip next row, work first half of another dc in end of next row, yo, pull through 3 lps on hook) around, join with sl st in top of first dc. Fasten off. *(32 dc decreases)*

Bottom Edging

Hold Cover with top pointing down; working in ends of rows around bottom edge, with No. 0 hook, join yarn with sc in any row, ch 3, (dc, ch 1, dc, ch 1) in each row around, join with sl st in second ch of ch-3. Fasten off.

PINEAPPLE LACE
Top Band

Row 1: With No. 7 hook and single strand size 10 cotton thread, ch 8, sl st in third ch from hook, skip next 3 chs, 2 dc in next ch, ch 3, dc in last ch, turn.

Rows 2-32: Ch 5, dc in ch-3 sp of last row, ch 3, sl st in **front lp and left bar** of dc *(see illustration)*, (2 dc, ch 3, 3 dc) in same ch sp, turn. At end of last row, join with sl st in top of ch-3 at beginning of row 1. Fasten off.

Tack ch-3 sp on last row to bottom of row 1.

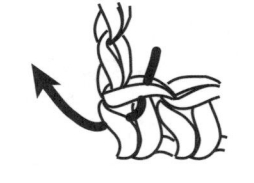

Edging

Rnd 1: Working around one edge of Top Band, with No. 7 hook and single strand size 10 cotton thread, join with sc in any ch-5 sp, (ch 5, sc in next ch-5 sp) around, ch 3, tr in first sc.

Rnd 2: (Ch 3, sc in next ch sp) around, ch 2, dc in top of tr.

Rnd 3: (Ch 2, sc in next ch sp) around, ch 1, hdc in top of dc.

Rnd 4: Ch 5, (tr, ch 1, tr) in next ch sp, *ch 1, tr in next ch sp, ch 1, (tr, ch 1, tr) in next ch sp; repeat from * around, ch 1, join with sl st in fourth ch of beginning ch-5.

Rnd 5: Sc in next ch-1 sp, ch 3, work (dc, ch 3, sl st in front lp and left bar of dc, ch 1, dc) in same ch-1 sp, ch 1, work (dc, ch 1, dc, ch 3, sl st in front lp and left bar of dc, ch 1, dc, ch 1) in each ch-1 sp around, join with sl st in second ch of ch-3. Fasten off.

First Pineapple

Row 1: Working on opposite side of Top Band in ch-5 sps only, with No. 7 hook and single strand size 10 cotton thread, join with sc in any ch-5 sp, (ch 2, 2 dc, ch 3, 3 dc) in same ch sp, 10 tr in next ch-5 sp; for **shell, (3 dc, ch 3, 3 dc)** in next ch-5 sp, turn.

Row 2: Ch 1, sl st in next 2 sts, (sc, ch 2, 2 dc, ch 3, 3 dc) in next ch sp, sc in next 10 tr, shell in ch-3 sp of last shell, ch 5, sl st in top of ch-2, turn.

Row 3: Ch 1, (sc, ch 3, sc, ch 5, sc, ch 3, sc) in first ch-5 sp, sl st in next 3 dc, (sc, ch 2, 2 dc, ch 3, 3 dc) in next ch-3 sp, ch 1, sc in next sc, (ch 3, sc in next sc) 9 times, ch 1, shell in ch-3 sp of last shell, ch 5, sl st in top of ch-2, turn.

Row 4: Ch 1, (sc, ch 3, sc, ch 5, sc, ch 3, sc) in first ch-5 sp, sl st in next 3 dc, (sc, ch 2, 2 dc, ch 3, 3 dc) in next ch-3 sp, ch 2, skip next ch sp, sc in next ch-3 sp, (ch 3, sc in next ch-3 sp) 8 times, ch 2, skip next ch sp, shell in ch-3 sp of last shell, ch 5, sl st in top of ch-2, turn.

Row 5: Ch 1, (sc, ch 3, sc, ch 5,

sc, ch 3, sc) in first ch-5 sp, sl st in next 3 dc, (sc, ch 2, 2 dc, ch 3, 3 dc) in next ch-3 sp, ch 3, skip next ch sp, sc in next ch-3 sp, (ch 3, sc in next ch-3 sp) 7 times, ch 3, skip next ch sp, shell in ch-3 sp of last shell, ch 5, sl st in top of ch-2, turn.

Row 6: Ch 1, (sc, ch 3, sc, ch 5, sc, ch 3, sc) in first ch-5 sp, sl st in next 3 dc, (sc, ch 2, 2 dc, ch 3, 3 dc) in next ch-3 sp, ch 4, skip next ch sp, sc in next ch-3 sp, (ch 3, sc in next ch-3 sp) 6 times, ch 4, skip next ch sp, shell in ch-3 sp of last shell, ch 5, sl st in top of ch-2, turn.

Row 7: Ch 1, (sc, ch 3, sc, ch 5, sc, ch 3, sc) in first ch-5 sp, sl st in next 3 dc, (sc, ch 2, 2 dc, ch 3, 3 dc) in next ch-3 sp, ch 5, skip next ch sp, sc in next ch-3 sp, (ch 3, sc in next ch-3 sp) 5 times, ch 5, skip next ch sp, shell in ch-3 sp of last shell, ch 5, sl st in top of ch-2, turn.

Row 8: Ch 1, (sc, ch 3, sc, ch 5, sc, ch 3, sc) in first ch-5 sp, sl st in next 3 dc, (sc, ch 2, 2 dc, ch 3, 3 dc) in next ch-3 sp, ch 6, skip next ch sp, sc in next ch-3 sp, (ch 3, sc in next ch-3 sp) 4 times, ch 6, skip next ch sp, shell in ch-3 sp of last shell, ch 5, sl s tin top of ch-2, turn.

Row 9: Ch 1, (sc, ch 3, sc, ch 5, sc, ch 3, sc) in first ch-5 sp, sl st in next 3 dc, (sc, ch 2, 2 dc, ch 3, 3 dc) in next ch-3 sp, ch 7, skip next ch sp, sc in next ch-3 sp, (ch 3, sc in next ch-3 sp) 3 times, ch 7, skip next ch sp, shell in ch-3 sp of last shell, ch 5, sl st in top of ch-2, turn.

Row 10: Ch 1, (sc, ch 3, sc, ch 5, sc, ch 3, sc) in first ch-5 sp, sl st in next 3 dc, (sc, ch 2, 2 dc, ch 3, 3 dc) in next ch-3 sp, ch 8, skip next ch sp, sc in next ch-3 sp, (ch 3, sc in next ch-3 sp) 2 times, ch 8, skip next ch sp, shell in ch-3 sp of last shell, ch 5, sl st in top of ch-2, turn.

Row 11: Ch 1, (sc, ch 3, sc, ch 5, sc, ch 3, sc) in first ch-5 sp, sl st in next 3 dc, (sc, ch 2, 2 dc, ch 3 dc) in next ch-3 sp, ch 8, skip next ch sp, sc in next ch-3 sp, ch 3, sc in next ch-3 sp, ch 8, skip next ch sp, shell in ch-3 sp of last shell, ch 5, sl st in top of ch-2, turn.

Row 12: Ch 1, (sc, ch 3, sc, ch 5, sc, ch 3, sc) in first ch-5 sp, sl st in next 3 dc, (sc, ch 2, 2 dc, ch 3, 3 dc) in next ch-3 sp, ch 8, skip next ch sp, sc in next ch-3 sp, ch 8, skip next ch sp, shell in ch-3 sp of last shell, ch 5, sl st in top of ch-2, turn.

Row 13: Ch 1, (sc, ch 3, sc, ch 5, sc, ch 3, sc) in first ch-5 sp, sl st in next 3 dc, (sc, ch 2, 2 dc, ch 3, 3 dc) in next ch-3 sp, skip next 2 ch sps, shell in ch-3 sp of last shell, ch 5, sl st in top of ch-2, turn.

Row 14: Ch 1, (sc, ch 3, sc, ch 5, sc, ch 3, sc) in first ch-5 sp, sl st in next dc, ch 5, sl st in top of ch-2, turn.

Row 15: Ch 1, (sl st, ch 3, dc) in first ch-5 sp; for **picot, ch 3, sl st in third ch from hook, ch 5, sl st in fifth ch from hook, ch 3, sl st in third ch from hook, sl st in first ch on first ch-3 of picot;** (4 dc, picot, 5 dc, picot, dc) in same ch-5 sp. Fasten off.

Second Pineapple

Skip next ch-5 sp on edge of Top Band and work First Pineapple in next 3 ch-5 sps.

Working between Pineapples, join with sc in ch-5 sp made at beginning of row 4 on First Pineapple, ch 3, sc in skipped ch-5 sp on Top Band, ch 3, sc in ch-5 sp made at beginning of row 3 on second Pineapple, **turn;** ch 8, sl st in first sc, **turn;** work (5 sc, picot, 5 sc) in ch-8 sp just made, join with sl st in sc worked in to sp at beginning of row 3. Fasten off.

Third & Fourth Pineapples

Work same as Second Pineapple.

FINISHING

Tack ch-2 sps of rnd 3 on Lace Edging to Top Opening of Cover. Weave ribbon through sts of rnd 4 on Lace Edging, going under 2 and over 1. Tie ends in bow.◻◻

Valance

Designed by Addie May Bodwell

FINISHED SIZE:
39" across.

MATERIALS:
- ❏ 260 yds. size 10 crochet cotton thread
- ❏ No. 8 steel hook or hook size needed to obtain gauge

GAUGE:
9 sts = 1"; dtr = ⅝" tall.

BASIC STITCHES:
Ch, sl st, sc, dc, tr, dtr.

NOTE:
A bullion stitch may be substituted for (dtr, ch 1).

SPECIAL STITCH:
For **bullion stitch,** yo 20 times, insert hook in st, yo, pull lp through st, yo, pull through all 21 lps on hook at same time (if pulling through all lps in difficult, try pulling hook through 1 or 2 lps at a time until all lps have been worked off), ch 1. If making this stitch for the first time, practice before starting instructions.

VALANCE

Row 1: Ch 338, dc in fourth ch from hook, dc in each ch across, turn. *(336 dc made) Front of row 1 is right side of work.*

Row 2: Ch 1, sc in first st, (ch 7, skip next 4 sts, sc in next st) across, making 67 lps in all, turn.

Row 3: Ch 5, (tr, ch 6, tr) in first ch lp, *ch 5, tr in next ch lp, ch 5, dc in next ch lp, ch 5, (tr, ch 6, tr) in next ch lp; repeat from * across, ending with ch 5, join with sl st in first sc, **do not turn.** Fasten off.

Note: All following rows are fastened off at the end of the row and worked on the right side only; do not turn at the end of these rows.

Row 4: Join with sl st in first ch-6 lp at beginning of last row, ch 5; for **beginning of first pineapple, (dtr—*see Stitch Guide*, ch 1) 8 times in same ch lp;** *ch 6, (dtr, ch 1) 4 times in next ch-6 lp, ch 6; for **beginning of next pineapple, (dtr, ch 1) 8 times in next ch-6 lp;** repeat from * across, ending with dtr in top of last ch-5.

Row 5: Join with sc between first 2 dtr of first pineapple, (ch 5, sc between next 2 dtr) 6 times *(making 6 ch lps in all),* *ch 7, (dtr, ch 1) 4 times in ch sp between second and third dtr of next 4 dtr of last row, ch 6, sc between first 2 dtr of next pineapple, (ch 5, sc between next 2 dtr) 6 times; repeat from * across.

Row 6: Join with sc in first ch lp of first pineapple, (ch 5, sc in next ch lp) 5 times, *ch 7, (dtr, ch 1) 4 times in ch lp between second and third dtr of next 4 dtr, ch 6, sc in first ch lp of next pineapple, (ch 5, sc in next ch lp) 5 times; repeat from * across.

Row 7: Join with sc in first ch lp of first pineapple, (ch 5, sc in next ch lp) 4 times, *ch 7, (dtr, ch 1) 6 times in ch lps between second and third dtr of next 4 dtr, ch 6, sc in first ch lp of next pineapple, (ch 5, sc in next ch lp) 4 times.

Row 8: Join with sc in first ch lp of first pineapple, (ch 5, sc in next ch lp) 3 times, *ch 7, (dtr, ch 1) 4 times in ch lp between second and third dtr of next 6 dtr, ch 6, (dtr, ch 1) 4 times between fourth and fifth dtr of same 6 dtr, ch 6, sc in first ch lp of next pineapple, (ch 5, sc in next ch lp) 3 times; repeat from * across.

Row 9: Join with sc in first ch lp of first pineapple, (ch 5, sc in next ch lp) 2 times, *ch 7, (dtr, ch 1) 4 times in ch lp between second and third dtr of next 4 dtr, ch 4, (tr, ch 6, tr) in next ch-7 lp, ch 5, (dtr, ch 1) 4 times in ch lp between second and third dtr of next 4 dtr, ch 6, sc in first ch lp of next pineapple, (ch 5, sc in next ch lp) 2 times; repeat from * across.

Row 10: Join with sc in first ch lp of first pineapple, ch 5, sc in next ch lp, *ch 7, (dtr, ch 1) 4 times in ch lp between second and third dtr of next 4 dtr, ch 5, (dtr, ch 1) 8 times in ch-6 lp between next 2 tr, ch 5, (dtr, ch 1) 4 times in ch lp between second and third dtr of next 4 dtr, ch 6, sc in first ch lp of next pineapple, ch 5, sc in next ch lp; repeat from * across.

Row 11: For **edging,** with right side facing you, beginning at outer edge of first pineapple, join with sc in beginning ch at bottom of first dc, ch 7, sc in first ch lp of second row, ch 7, sc in ch-5 lp at beginning of fourth row, ch 7, sc in first ch lp of fifth row, ch 7, sc in first ch lp of eighth row, ch 7, sc in center of ch lp at point of pineapple, *ch 7, sc in center of next ch-7 lp, ch 7, sc in ch lp between second and third dtr of next 4 dtr, ch 7, sc in next ch-5 lp, (ch 7, skip next 2 dtr, sc in next ch lp between dtr) 3 times, ch 7, sc in next ch-5 lp, ch 7, sc in ch lp between second and third dtr of next 4 dtr, ch 7, sc in center of next ch-7 lp, ch 7, sc in center of ch lp at point of next pineapple; repeat from * across to last pineapple; work down side of last pineapple in same manner as first pineapple, ending with sc in beginning ch at bottom of last dc.

Row 12: Join with sc in first ch-7 lp of row 11, (4 sc, ch 3, 5 sc) in same ch lp, (5 sc, ch 3, 5 sc) in each ch-7 lp around. Fasten off. ❑❑

Purse

Designed by Mary L. Barton

FINISHED SIZE:
7½" tall.

MATERIALS:
- ❑ 605 yds. size 10 crochet cotton thread
- ❑ ⅓ yd. fabric
- ❑ Sewing thread to match fabric
- ❑ Sewing needle
- ❑ No. 8 steel hook or hook size needed to obtain gauge

GAUGE:
8 sts = 1"; bullion stitch = ½" tall

BASIC STITCHES:
Ch, sl st, sc, dc, tr, dtr.

NOTE:
A (tr, ch 1) can be substituted for the bullion stitch if desired.

SPECIAL STITCH:
For **bullion stitch (bs)**, yo 15 times, insert hook in st, yo, pull lp through st, yo, pull through all 16 lps on hook at same time (if pulling through all lps is difficult, try pulling hook through 1 or 2 lps at a time until all lps have been worked off), ch 1. If making this stitch for the first time, practice before starting instructions.

PURSE
Rnd 1: Ch 5, sl st in first ch to form ring, ch 5, **bs** (see Special Stitch) in ring, (ch 3, bs) 9 times, ch 3, join with sl st in top of ch-5. (10 bs, 10 ch sps made)
Rnd 2: Ch 5, (bs, ch 2, bs, ch 2) in each ch-3 sp around, join. (20 bs, 20 ch sps)
Rnd 3: Ch 5, (bs, ch 1, bs, ch 1) in each ch-2 sp around, join. (40 bs, 40 ch sps)
Rnd 4: Ch 5, 2 bs in each ch-1 sp around, join. (80 bs)
Rnd 5: Ch 5, skip first 2 bs, (sc in next sp between bs, ch 5, skip next 2 bs) around, join with sl st in joining sl st of last rnd. (40 ch sps)
Rnd 6: Sl st in first 3 chs of first ch-5, ch 3, (dc, ch 3, dc) in next ch sp, ch 3, *sc in next ch sp, ch 3, (dc, ch 3, dc) in next ch sp, ch 3; repeat from * around, join with sl st in third sl st. (60 ch -3 sps)
Rnd 7: Sl st in next 3 chs and in next dc, sl st in next ch sp, ch 5, 4 bs in same ch sp, ch 5, skip next 2 ch sps, 6 bs in next ch sp, ch 5, skip next 2 ch sps, (4 bs in next ch sp, ch 5, skip next 2 ch sps, 6 bs in next ch sp, ch 5, skip next 2 ch sps) around, join with sl st in top of first ch-5. (100 bs, 20 ch sps)
Rnd 8: Ch 5, *bs in next 4 bs, ch 5, skip next ch sp and next bs, sc in next sp between bs, (ch 3, sc in next sp between bs) 4 times, ch 5, skip next bs; repeat from * around, join. (40 bs, 60 ch sps)
Rnd 9: Sl st in next 2 bs, ch 5, *4 bs in next sp between bs, ch 5, skip next 2 bs and next ch sp, sc in next ch sp, (ch 3, sc in next ch sp) 3 times, ch 5, skip next ch sp and next 2 bs; repeat from * around, join. (40 bs, 50 ch sps)
Rnd 10: Ch 5, skip next bs, *4 bs in next sp between bs, skip next sp between bs, 4 bs in next sp between bp, ch 5, skip next ch sp, sc in next ch sp, (ch 3, sc in next ch sp) 2 times, ch 5, skip next ch sp and next bs; repeat from * around, join. (80 bs, 50 ch sps)
Rnd 11: Sl st in next 2 bs, ch 5, (4 bs in next sp between bs, ch 5, skip next 3 sps between bs, 4 bs in next sp between bs, ch 5, skip next ch sp, sc in next ch sp, ch 3, sc in next ch sp, ch 5, skip next ch sp and next 2 bs) around, join. (80 bs, 40 ch sps)
Rnd 12: Sl st in next 2 bs, ch 5, *4 bs in next sp between bs, ch

3, (dtr, ch 3, dtr) in next ch sp, ch 3, skip next 2 bs, 4 bs in next sp between bs, ch 5, skip next ch sp, sc in next ch sp, ch 5, skip next ch sp and next 2 bs; repeat from * around, join. *(80 bs, 50 ch sps, 20 dtr)*

Rnd 13: Sl st in next 2 bs, ch 5, (4 bs in next sp between bs, ch 5, skip next 2 bs and next ch sp, 6 bs in next ch sp, ch 5, skip next ch sp and next 2 bs, 4 bs in next sp between bs, skip next 4 bs and next 2 ch sps) around, join. *(140 bs, 20 ch sps)*

Rnd 14: Sl st in next 2 bs, ch 5, *4 bs in next sp between bs, ch 5, skip next ch sp and bs, sc in next sp between bs, (ch 3, skip next bs, sc in next sp between bs) 4 times, ch 5, skip next ch sp and next 2 bs, 4 bs in next sp between bs, skip next 4 bs; repeat from * around, join. *(80 bs, 60 ch sps)*

Rnd 15: Sl st in next 2 bs, ch 5, *4 bs in next sp between bs, ch 5, skip next 2 bs and next ch sp, sc in next ch sp, (ch 3, sc in next ch sp) 3 times, ch 5, skip next ch sp and next 2 bs, 4 bs in next sp between bs, skip next 4 bs; repeat from * around, join. *(80 bs, 50 ch sps)*

Rnd 16: Sl st in next 2 bs, ch 5, *4 bs in next sp between bp, ch 5, skip next 2 bs and next ch sp, sc in next ch sp, (ch 3, sc in next ch sp) 2 times, ch 5, skip next ch sp and next 2 bs, 4 bs in next sp between bs, skip next 4 bs; repeat from * around, join. *(80 bs, 40 ch sps)*

Rnd 17: Sl st in next 2 bs, ch 5, (4 bs in next sp between bs, ch 5, skip next 2 bs and next ch sp, sc in next ch sp, ch 3, sc in next ch sp, ch 5, skip next ch sp and next bs, 4 bs in next sp between bs, ch 5, skip next 4 bs) around, join.

Rnd 18: Sl st in next 2 bs, ch 5, *4 bs in next sp between bs, ch 5, skip next 2 bs and next ch sp, sc in next ch sp, ch 5, skip next ch sp and next 2 bs, 4 bs in next sp between bs, ch 3, (dtr, ch 3, dtr) in next ch sp, ch 3, skip next

2 bs; repeat from * around, join. *(80 bs, 50 ch sps, 20 dtr)*

Rnd 19: Sl st in next 2 bs, ch 5, (4 bs in next sp between bs, skip next 4 bs and next 2 ch sps, 4 bs in next sp between bs, ch 5, skip next 2 bs and next ch sp, 6 bs in next ch sp, ch 5, skip next ch sp and next 2 bs) around, join. *(140 bs, 20 ch sps)*

Rnd 20: Sl st in next 2 bs, ch 5, *4 bs in next sp between bs, skip next 4 bs, 4 bs in next sp between bs, ch 5, skip next 3 bs and ch sp, sc in next sp between bs, (ch 3, sc in next sp between bs) 4 times, ch 5, skip next 3 bs and next ch sp; repeat from * around, join. *(80 bs, 60 ch sps)*

Rnd 21: Sl st in next 2 bs, ch 5, *4 bs in next sp between bs, skip next 4 bs, 4 bs in next sp between bs, ch 5, skip next 2 bs and next ch sp, sc in next ch sp, (ch 3, sc in next ch sp) 3 times, ch 5, skip next ch sp and next 2 bs; repeat from * around, join. *(80 bs, 50 ch sps)*

Rnd 22: Sl st in next 2 bs, ch 5, *4 bs in next sp between bs, skip next 4 bs, 4 bs in next sp between bs, ch 5, skip next 2 bs and next ch sp, sc in next ch sp, (ch 3, sc in next ch sp) 2 times, ch 5, skip next ch sp and next 2 bs; repeat from * around, join. *(80 bs, 40 ch sps)*

Rnd 23: Sl st in next 2 bs, ch 5, (4 bs in next sp between bs, skip next 4 bs, 4 bs in next sp between bs, ch 5, skip next 2 bs and next ch sp, sc in next ch sp, ch 3, sc in next ch sp, ch 5, skip next ch sp and next 2 bs) around, join. *(80 bs, 30 ch sps)*

Rnd 24: Sl st in next 2 bs, ch 5, (4 bs in next sp between bs, skip next 4 bs, 4 bs in next sp between bs, ch 5, skip next 2 bs and next ch sp, sc in next ch sp, ch 5, skip next ch sp and next 2 bs) around, join. *(80 bs, 20 ch sps)*

Rnd 25: Sl st in next 2 bs, ch 5, 4 bs in next sp between bs, skip next 4 bs, (4 bs in next sp between bs, skip next 4 bs) around, join. *(80 bs)*

Rnd 26: Ch 7, skip next 2 bs, (tr in next sp between bs, ch 3, skip next 2 bs) around, join with sl st in fourth ch of ch-7. *(40 ch sps)*

Rnd 27: Ch 5, 2 bs in each ch sp around, join with sl st in top of ch-5. *(80 bs)*

Rnd 28: Ch 5, skip next 2 bs, (sc in next sp between bs, ch 5, skip next 2 bs) around, join with sl st in joining sl st of last rnd. *(40 ch sps)*

Rnd 29: Sl st in first 3 chs, ch 1, sc in same ch sp; for **picot, ch 4, sl st in front lp and left bar top of last st** *(see illustration)*; (2 dc, picot, 2 dc, picot, 2 dc) in next ch sp, *sc in next ch sp, picot, (2 dc, picot, 2 dc, picot, 2 dc) in next ch sp; repeat from * around, join with sl st in first sc. Fasten off.

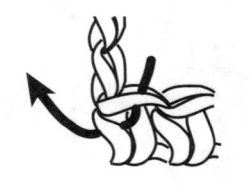

DRAWSTRING (make 2)
Ch 4, sl st in first ch to form ring, ch 2, (dc in each ch or st) around, **do not join**; repeat between ( ) around until cord is length of Purse, plus 2". Fasten off.

LINING
From fabric, cut two circles 6" in diameter for Bottom; cut one piece 10" x 24" for Side.

Sew 10" edges of Sides right sides together. Turn one 24" edge under ¼", turn under ¼" again and hem. Run gathering thread ¼" from other 24" edge; gather to 6" in diameter. Sew right side of one Bottom piece to inside of Side piece along gathered edge. Turn edge under ¼" on other Bottom piece and press; sew to outside of Side piece over seam of first Bottom piece.

Insert Lining in Purse. Sew top edge of Lining to top of sts on rnd 25 of Purse; weave Drawstrings through ch sps of rnd 26.

Sew ends of each Drawstring together.❏❏

Sweater & Cap

Designed by Una Bjork

FINISHED SIZES:
Infant's 0-3 mos. Finished measurement: 18" chest.
Infant's 6-9 mos. Finished measurement: 20" chest.

MATERIALS:
- 5 oz. fingering weight yarn
- 1½" square piece cardboard
- Tapestry needle
- Hook stated in gauges given or hook size needed to obtain gauge

GAUGE:
For 0-3 mos., using No. 4 steel hook, 2 shells = 1"; 7 shell rows = 2".
For 6-9 mos., using No. 3 steel hook, 7 shells = 4"; 3 shell rows = 1".

BASIC STITCHES:
Ch, sl st, sc, dc, tr.

SPECIAL STITCHES:
For **beginning shell (beg shell),** sl st in first 2 sts, (sl st, ch 3, dc, ch 1, 2 dc) in next ch sp.

For **shell,** (2 dc, ch 1, 2 dc) in specified sp or ch sp.

For **pineapple (p-apl),** ch 2, skip next ch sp, sc in next ch sp, (ch 3, sc in next ch sp) across to last ch sp before next shell or 2-dc group, ch 2, skip next ch sp.

For **V stitch (V st),** (dc, ch 1, dc) in specified ch sp.

SWEATER
Row 1: Ch 100, dc in fourth ch from hook, (ch 2, skip next 2 chs, dc in next 2 chs) across, turn. *(50 dc, 24 ch sps made)*

Row 2: Sl st in sp between first 2 sts, (ch 3, dc, ch 1, 2 dc) in same sp, *skip next ch sp, **shell** *(see Special Stitches)* in sp between next 2 sts; repeat from * across, turn. *(25 shells)*

Row 3: Beg shell *(see Special Stitches)*, shell in ch sp of each shell across, turn.

Row 4: Beg shell, (ch 2, 5 tr in next shell, ch 2, shell in next shell) across, turn.

Row 5: Beg shell, *[ch 2, dc in next tr, (ch 1, dc in next tr) 4 times, ch 2], (2 dc, ch 1, shell) in next shell; repeat from * 10 more times; repeat between [ ], shell in last shell, turn.

Row 6: Beg shell, [*p-apl *(see Special Stitches)*, shell in next shell], ch 2, shell in next ch sp; repeat from * 10 more times; repeat between [ ], turn.

Row 7: Beg shell, (p-apl, shell in next shell, ch 1, shell in next ch sp, ch 1, shell in next shell) 11 times, p-apl, shell in last shell, turn.

Row 8: Beg shell, (p-apl, shell in next shell, ch 2, 7 tr in next shell, ch 2, shell in next shell) across to last pineapple, p-apl, shell in last shell, turn.

Row 9: Beg shell, *[skip next ch sp, dc in next ch sp, shell in next shell], ch 2, dc in next tr, (ch 1, dc in next tr) 6 times, ch 2, shell in next shell; repeat from * across to last pineapple; repeat between [ ], turn.

Row 10: Beg shell, (ch 1, shell in next shell, p-apl, shell in next shell) across to last shell, ch 1, shell in last shell, turn.

Row 11: Sl st in next 2 sts, sl st in next ch sp, ch 3, **V st** *(see Special Stitches)* in same ch sp, *[ch 1, V st in next ch-1 sp, ch 1, (v st, dc) in next shell], p-apl, (dc, V st) in next shell; repeat from * across to last shell; repeat

Row 12: Beg shell, *(ch 2, shell in ch sp of next V st) 2 times, p-apl, shell in ch sp of next V st; repeat from * across to last 2 V sts; repeat between ( ) 2 times, turn.

Row 13: Beg shell, (*ch 2, 7 tr in next shell, ch 2, shell in next shell*, p-apl, shell in next shell) across to last 2 shells; repeat between **, turn.

Row 14: Beg shell, *[ch 2, dc in next tr, ch 1, dc in next tr) 6 times, ch 2, shell in next shell], p-apl, shell in next shell; repeat from * across to last 7-tr group; repeat between [ ], turn.

Row 15: Beg shell, *(p-apl, shell in next shell), skip next ch sp, dc in next ch sp, shell in next shell*; repeat between ( ); [for **armhole,** yo, skip next ch sp, insert hook in ch sp at top of next pineapple, yo, pull lp through, yo, pull through 2 lps on hook, skip next 4 shells and 3 pineapples, yo, insert hook in ch sp at top of next pineapple, yo, pull lp through, yo, pull through 2 lps on hook, yo, pull through all 3 lps on hook, mark this stitch; shell in next shell; repeat between ** 3 more times; repeat between ( ); repeat between [ ]; shell in next shell; repeat between **; repeat between ( ), turn.

Row 16: Beg shell, (p-apl, shell in next shell, ch 1, shell in next shell) 7 times, p-apl, shell in last shell, turn.

Row 17: Beg shell, *p-apl, (dc, V st) in next shell, ch 1, V st in next ch-1 sp, ch 1, (V st, dc) in next shell; repeat from * 6 more times, p-apl, shell in last shell, turn.

Row 18: B eg shell, *p-apl, (shell in next V st, ch 2) 2 times, shell in next V st; repeat from * 6 more times, p-apl, shell in last shell, turn.

Rows 19-25: Repeat rows 8-14.

Row 26: Beg shell, (p-apl, shell in next shell, skip next ch sp, dc in next ch sp, shell in next shell) 7 times, p-apl, shell in last shell, turn.

Row 27: Beg shell, p-apl, shell in next shell leaving remaining sts unworked, turn. Mark last shell worked in.

Rows 28-30: For **first point,** beg shell, p-apl, shell in last shell, turn.

Row 31: Beg shell, skip next ch sp, dc in next ch sp, shell in last shell, turn.

Row 32: Sl st in first 2 sts, ch 1, sc in next ch sp, ch 1, shell in next st, ch 1, sc in last shell, turn. Fasten off.

Row 27: For **second point,** join with sl st in marked shell on row 26, sl st in ch sp of next unworked shell, (ch 3, dc, ch 1, 2 dc) in same ch sp, p-apl, shell in next shell, turn. Mark last shell worked in.

Rows 28-32: Repeat rows 28-32 of first point.

For **remaining points,** repeat second point 6 more times.

Sleeves

Rnd 1: Join with sl st in shell on right-hand side of center underarm, (ch 3, dc, ch 1, 2 dc) in same ch sp, **dc around post** *(see Stitch Guide)* of marked st on row 15, *shell in next shell, p-apl*, shell in next shell, skip next ch sp, dc in next ch sp; repeat between **, join with sl st in top of ch-3, sl st in next st and in next ch sp, **turn.**

Rnd 2: (Ch 3, dc, ch 1, 2 dc) in same ch sp, *p-apl, shell in next shell, ch 2*, shell in next shell; repeat between **, join, sl st in next st and in next ch sp, **turn.**

Rnd 3: (Ch 3, V st) in same ch sp, *ch 2, V st in next ch sp, ch 2, (V st, dc) in next shell, p-apl*, (dc, V st) in next shell; repeat between **, join, sl st in next st and in next ch sp, **turn.**

Rnd 4: (Ch 3, dc, ch 1, 2 dc) in same ch sp, *p-apl, shell in next V st, (ch 3, shell in next V st)* 2 times; repeat between **, join, sl st in next st and in next ch sp, **turn.**

Rnd 5: (Ch 3, dc, ch 1, 2 dc) in same ch sp, *ch 3, 7 tr in next shell, ch 3, shell in next shell, p-apl*, shell in next shell; repeat between **, join, sl st in next st and in next ch sp, **turn.**

Rnd 6: (Ch 3, dc, ch 1, 2 dc) in same ch sp, *skip next ch sp, dc in next ch sp, shell in next shell,

ch 3, dc in next tr, (ch 1, dc in next tr) 6 times, ch 3*, shell in next shell; repeat between **, join, sl st in next st and in next ch sp, **turn.**

Rnd 7: (Ch 3, dc, ch 1, 2 dc) in same ch sp, *p-apl, shell in next shell, ch 3*, shell in next shell; repeat between **, join, sl st in next st and in next ch sp, **turn.**

Rnds 8-10: Repeat rnds 3-5.

Rnd 11: (Ch 3, dc, ch 1, 2 dc) in same ch sp, *p-apl, shell in next shell, ch 3, dc in next tr, (ch 1, dc in next tr) 6 times, ch 3*, shell in next shell; repeat between **, join, sl st in next st and in next ch sp, **turn.**

Rnd 12: (Ch 3, dc, ch 1, 2 dc) in same ch sp, *p-apl, shell in next shell, skip next ch sp, dc in next ch sp*, shell in next shell; repeat between **, join, sl st in next st and in next ch sp, turn.

Rnd 13: (Ch 3, dc, ch 1, 2 dc) in same ch sp, *ch 3, shell in next shell, p-apl*, shell in next shell; repeat between **, join, sl st in next st and in next ch sp, **turn.**

Rnd 14: (Ch 4, 2 dc) in same ch sp, *p-apl, (dc, V st) in next shell, ch 2, V st in next ch sp, ch 2*, (V st, dc) in next shell; repeat between **, join with sl st in third ch of ch-4, sl st in next ch sp, **turn.**

Rnd 15: (Ch 3, dc, ch 1, 2 dc) in same ch sp, *(ch 3, shell in next V st) 2 times, p-apl*, shell in next V st; repeat between **, join with sl st in top of ch-3, sl st in next st and in next ch sp, **turn.**

Rnd 16: (Ch 3, dc, ch 1, 2 dc) in same ch sp, *p-apl, shell in next shell, ch 3, 7 tr in next shell, ch 3*, shell in next shell; repeat between **, join, sl st in next st and in next ch sp, **turn.**

Rnd 17: (Ch 3, dc, ch 1, 2 dc) in same ch sp, *ch 3, dc in next tr, (ch 1, dc in next tr) 6 times, ch 3, shell in next shell, skip next ch sp, dc in next ch sp*, shell in next shell; repeat between **, join, sl st in next st and in next ch sp, **turn.**

Rnd 18: Ch 1, sc in same ch sp, *shell in next dc, sc in next shell, p-apl*, sc in next shell; repeat between **, join with sl st in first sc. Fasten off.

Repeat on other armhole.

For **tie,** make chain 24" long. Fasten off. Weave through ch sps on rnd 1.

Pom-pom (make 2)

Wrap yarn around cardboard 150 times; slide loops off cardboard; tie separate 6" strand yarn tightly around center of all loops; cut loops. Trim ends.

Sew one to each end of tie.

CAP

Rnd 1: Starting at back, ch 4, sl st in first ch to form ring, ch 3, 11 dc in ring, join with sl st in top of ch-3. *(12 dc made)*

Rnd 2: (Ch 3, dc) in first st, 2 dc in each st around, join, **turn.** *(24)*

Rnd 3: (Ch 3, dc) in first st, dc in next st, (2 dc in next st, dc in next st) around, join. *(36)*

Rnd 4: (Ch 3, dc) in first st, dc in next 2 sts, (2 dc in next st, dc in next 2 sts) around, join, **turn.** *(48)*

Rnds 5-6: (Ch 3, dc) in first st, dc in next 3 sts, (2 dc in next st, dc in next 3 sts) around, join. At end of last rnd, turn. *(75)*

Rnd 7: Ch 3, dc in each st around, join.

Row 8: Working in rows, (ch 3, dc, ch 1, 2 dc) in first st, (skip next 3 sts, shell in next st) 12 times leaving last 26 sts unworked, turn. *(13 shells)*

Row 9: Beg shell, (ch 1, shell in next shell) across, turn.

Row 10: Beg shell, (ch 2, shell in next shell) across, turn.

Row 11: Beg shell, (ch 2, 5 tr in next shell, ch 2, shell in next shell) across, turn.

Row 12: Beg shell, *[ch 2, dc in next tr, (ch 1, dc in next tr) 4 times, ch 2], (2 dc, ch 1, shell) in next shell; repeat from * 4 more times; repeat between [ ], shell in last shell, turn.

Row 13: Beg shell, (p-apl, shell in next shell, ch 1, shell in next ch sp) 5 times, p-apl, shell in last shell, turn.

Row 14: Beg shell, (p-apl, shell in next shell, shell in next ch-1 sp, shell in next shell) 5 times, p-apl, shell in last shell, turn.

Row 15: Beg shell, (p-apl, shell in next shell, ch 2, 5 tr in next shell, ch 2, shell in next shell) 5 times, p-apl, shell in last shell, turn.

Row 16: Beg shell, *[skip next ch sp, dc in next ch sp, shell in next shell], ch 2, dc in next tr, (ch 1, dc in next tr) 4 times, ch 2, shell in next shell; repeat from * 4 more times; repeat between [ ], turn.

Row 17: Beg shell, (ch 1, shell in next shell, p-apl, shell in next shell) 5 times, ch 1, shell in last shell, turn.

Row 18: Beg shell, (*V st in next ch sp, shell in next shell*, p-apl, shell in next shell) 5 times; repeat between **, turn.

Row 19: Beg shell, (*shell in next V st, shell in next shell*, p-apl, shell in next shell) 5 times; repeat between **, turn.

Row 20: Beg shell, (*ch 2, 5 tr in next shell, ch 2, shell in next shell*, skip next ch sp, dc in next ch sp, shell in next shell) 5 times; repeat between **, turn.

Row 21: Beg shell, *[ch 2, dc in next tr, (ch 1, dc in next tr) 4 times, ch 2, shell in next shell], ch 1, shell in next shell; repeat from * 4 more times; repeat between [ ], turn.

Row 22: Beg shell, (p-apl, shell in next shell, V st in next ch-1 sp, shell in next shell) 5 times, p-apl, shell in last shell, turn.

Row 23: Beg shell, (p-apl, shell in next shell, shell in next V st, shell in next shell) 5 times, p-apl, shell in last shell, turn.

Rows 24-25: Repeat rows 15-16.

Row 26: Sl st in first 2 sts, ch 1, sc in next ch sp, (*shell in next dc, sc in next shell*, p-apl, sc in next shell) 5 times; repeat between **, sl st in last 2 sts of last shell, **do not turn.**

Rnd 27: For **edging,** working around outer edge, 2 sc in end of next 18 rows, sc in each unworked st on row 7, 2 sc in end of next 18 rows; working across front, sc in next 2 sl sts, *sc in next 3 sts, (sc, ch 3, sc) in next ch sp, sc in next 3 sts, ch 1, skip next ch sp, (sc in next ch sp, ch 3) 2 times, sc in next ch sp, ch 1, skip next ch sp; repeat from * 5 more times, sc in next 3 sts, (sc, ch 3, sc) in next ch sp, sc in next 3 sts, sc in last 2 sl sts, join with sl st in first sc.

Row 28: Ch 3, dc in next st, (ch 2, skip next 2 sts, dc in next 2 sts) 24 times. Fasten off.

Pom-Pom (make 2)

Work same as Sweater pom-pom. For **tie,** make chain 18" long. Fasten off. Weave through sts on row 28.❏❏

Elegant Afghan

Designed by Ann Emery Smith

FINISHED SIZE:
44½" x 66".

MATERIALS:
❑ 32 oz. off-white worsted yarn
❑ Tapestry needle

❑ H hook or hook size needed to obtain gauge

GAUGE:
7 sc = 2", 6 sc **back lp** rows = 1¾".

BASIC STITCHES:
Ch, sl st, sc, dc, tr.

SPECIAL STITCHES:
For **cluster,** yo, insert hook in next st, yo, pull through st, yo, pull

through 2 lps on hook, yo, insert hook in same st, yo, pull through st, yo, pull through 2 lps on hook, yo, pull through all lps on hook.

For **Scallop joining,** drop lp from hook, insert hook in center st of corresponding 3-dc group on previous Scallop, pull dropped lp through.

For **dc joining,** ch 3 (not counted or used as a st), drop lp from hook, insert hook in end of corresponding dc row on previous Lacy Section, pull dropped lp through, ch 1.

For **shell,** (2 dc, ch 2, 2 dc) in next ch sp.

HALF (make 2)
First Scallop
Foundation: Ch 15, sl st in first ch to form ring, ch 1, 26 sc in ring, join with sl st in first sc. *(26 sc made)*

Row 1: Ch 5 *(counts as first dc and ch-2),* skip next st, (dc in next st, ch 2, skip next st) 5 times, (dc, ch 3, dc) in next st, (ch 2, skip next st, dc in next st) 6 times leaving last st unworked, turn. *(14 dc, 13 ch sps)* Front of row 1 is right side of work.

Row 2: Ch 1, sc in first st, (2 sc in next ch sp, sc in next st) 6 times, 3 sc in next ch sp, sc in next st, (2 sc in next ch sp, sc in next st) 6 times, turn. *(41 sc)*

Rows 3–7: Working these rows in **back lps** *(see Stitch Guide),* ch 1, skip first st, sc in next 19 sts, 3 sc in next st, sc in next 19 sts leaving last st unworked, turn.

Row 8: Working in **both lps,** (ch 3, dc) in first st, (ch 3, skip next 2 sts, **cluster**—*see Special Stitches*) 6 times, ch 3, skip next st, (cluster, ch 3, cluster) in next st, ch 3, skip next st, cluster in next st, (ch 3, skip next 2 sts, cluster) 6 times, turn. *(15 ch sps)*

Row 9: Ch 1, (sc, 3 dc, sc) in each ch sp across. Fasten off.

Second Scallop
Foundation: Ch 15, sl st in first ch to form ring, ch 1, 26 sc in ring, join with sl st in first sc. *(26 sc made)*

Rows 1–8: Repeat rows 1–8 of First Scallop.

Row 9: Ch 1, (sc, dc, work **Scallop joining**—*see Special Stitches,* 2 dc, sc) in each of first 2 ch sps, (sc, 3 dc, sc) in each ch sp across. Fasten off.

Third–Fifth Scallops
Work same as Second Scallop.

SECTION A
First Lacing
Row 1: With right side facing you, join with sl st in end of row 8 on last Scallop, (ch 3, 2 dc) in end of same row as joining sl st, ch 7, sc in end of row 4, ch 3, sc in end of row 2, ch 7, (2 dc, ch 2, 2 dc) in unworked st on Foundation (shell made), ch 7, sc in end of row 2 on other side, ch 3, sc in end of row 4, ch 7, 3 dc in end of row 8 leaving remaining Scallops unworked, turn. *(6 dc, 6 ch sps, 1 shell made)*

Row 2: (Ch 3, 2 dc) in first st, ch 3, sc in next ch-7 sp, ch 5, skip next ch-3 sp, sc in next ch-7 sp, ch 3, **shell** *(see Special Stitches)* in ch sp of next shell, ch 3, sc in next ch-7 sp, ch 5, skip next ch-3 sp, sc in next ch-7 sp, ch 3, 3 dc in last st, turn.

Row 3: (Ch 3, 2 dc) in first st, skip next ch-3 sp, 11 tr in next ch-5 sp, skip next ch-3 sp, shell in ch sp of next shell, skip next ch-3 sp, 11 tr in next ch-5 sp, skip next ch-3 sp, 3 dc in last st, turn.

Row 4: (Ch 3, 2 dc) in first st, ch 2, sc in first st of next 11-tr group, (ch 3, skip next st, sc in next st) 5 times, ch 2, shell in next shell, ch 2, sc in first st of next 11-tr group, (ch 3, skip next st, sc in next st) 5 times, ch 2, 3 dc in last st, turn.

Row 5: (Ch 3, 2 dc) in first st, ch 3, skip next ch-2 sp, sc in next ch-3 sp, (ch 3, sc in next ch-3 sp) 4 times, ch 3, skip next ch-2 sp, shell in next shell, ch 3, skip next ch-2 sp, sc in next ch-3 sp, (ch 3, sc in next ch-3 sp) 4 times, ch 3, skip

next ch-2 sp, 3 dc in last st, turn.

Row 6: (Ch 3, 2 dc) in first st, ch 4, skip next ch-3 sp, sc in next ch-3 sp, (ch 3, sc in next ch-3 sp) 3 times, ch 4, skip next ch-3 sp, shell in next shell, ch 4, skip next ch-3 sp, sc in next ch-3 sp, (ch 3, sc in next ch-3 sp) 3 times, ch 4, skip next ch-3 sp, 3 dc in last st, turn.

Row 7: (Ch 3, 2 dc) in first st, ch 5, skip next ch-4 sp, sc in next ch-3 sp, (ch 3, sc in next ch-3 sp) 2 times, ch 5, skip next ch-4 sp, shell in next shell, ch 5, skip next ch-4 sp, sc in next ch-3 sp, (ch 3, sc in next ch-3 sp) 2 times, ch 5, skip next ch-4 sp, 3 dc in last st, turn.

Row 8: (Ch 3, 2 dc) in first st, ch 7, skip next ch-5 sp, sc in next ch-3 sp, ch 3, sc in next ch-3 sp, ch 7, skip next ch-5 sp, shell in next shell, ch 7, skip next ch-5 sp, sc in next ch-3 sp, ch 3, sc in next ch-3 sp, ch 7, skip next ch-5 sp, 3 dc in last st, turn.

Row 9: (Ch 3, 2 dc) in first st, ch 3, sc in next ch-7 sp, ch 5, skip next ch-3 sp, sc in next ch-7 sp, ch 3, shell in next shell, ch 3, sc in next ch-7 sp, ch 5, skip next ch-3 sp, sc in next ch-7 sp, ch 3, 3 dc in last st, turn.

Row 10: (Ch 3, 2 dc) in first st, skip next ch-3 sp, 11 tr in next ch-5 sp, skip next ch-3 sp, shell in next shell, skip next ch-3 sp, 11 tr in next ch-5 sp, skip next ch-3 sp, 3 dc in last st, turn. Fasten off.

Second Lacing
Row 1: With right side facing you, join with sl st in end of row 8 on next Scallop, (work **dc joining**—*see Special Stitches,* 3 dc) in end of same row as joining sl st, ch 7, sc in end of row 4, ch 3, sc in end of row 2, ch 7, (2 dc, ch 2, 2 dc) in unworked st on Foundation (shell made), ch 7, sc in end of row 2 on other side, ch 3, sc in end of row 4, ch 7, 3 dc in end of row 8 leaving remaining Scallops unworked, turn. *(6 dc, 6 ch sps, 1 shell made)*

Row 2: (Ch 3, 2 dc) in first st, ch 3, sc in next ch-7 sp, ch 5, skip next ch-3 sp, sc in next ch-7 sp, ch 3, shell in ch sp of next shell, ch 3, sc in next ch-7 sp, ch 5, skip next ch-3 sp, sc in next ch-7 sp, ch 3, 3 dc in last st, turn.

Row 3: (Dc joining, 3 dc) in first st, skip next ch-3 sp, 11 tr in next ch-5 sp, skip next ch-3 sp, shell in ch sp of next shell, skip next ch-3 sp, 11 tr in next ch-5 sp, skip next ch-3 sp, 3 dc in last dc, turn.

Row 4: (Ch 3, 2 dc) in first st, ch 2, sc in first st of first 11-tr group, (ch 3, skip next st, sc in next st) 5 times, ch 2, shell in next shell, ch 2, sc in first st of next 11-tr group, (ch 3, skip next st, sc in next st) 5 times, ch 2, 3 dc in last dc, turn.

Row 5: (Dc joining, 3 dc) in first st, ch 3, skip next ch-2 sp, sc in next ch-3 sp, (ch 3, sc in next ch-3 sp) 4 times, ch 3, skip next ch-2 sp, shell in next shell, ch 3, skip next ch-2 sp, sc in next ch-3 sp, (ch 3, sc in next ch-3 sp) 4 times, ch 3, skip next ch-2 sp, 3 dc in last dc, turn.

Row 6: (Ch 3, 2 dc) in first st, ch 4, skip next ch-3 sp, sc in next ch-3 sp, (ch 3, sc in next ch-3 sp) 3 times, ch 4, skip next ch-3 sp, shell in next shell, ch 4, skip next ch-3 sp, sc in next ch-3 sp, (ch 3, sc in next ch-3 sp) 3 times, ch 4, skip next ch-3 sp, 3 dc in last dc, turn.

Row 7: (Dc joining, 3 dc) in first st, ch 5, skip next ch-4 sp, sc in next ch-3 sp, (ch 3, sc in next ch-3 sp) 2 times, ch 5, skip next ch-4 sp, shell in next shell, ch 5, skip next ch-4 sp, sc in next ch-3 sp, (ch 3, sc in next ch-3 sp) 2 times, ch 5, skip next ch-4 sp, 3 dc in last dc, turn.

Row 8: (Ch 3, 2 dc) in first st, ch 7, skip next ch-5 sp, sc in next ch-3 sp, ch 3, sc in next ch-3 sp, ch 7, skip next ch-5 sp, shell in next shell, ch 7, skip next ch-5 sp, sc in next ch-3 sp, ch 3, sc in next ch-3 sp, ch 7, skip next ch-5 sp, 3 dc in last dc, turn.

Row 9: (Dc joining, 3 dc) in first st, ch 3, sc in next ch-7 sp, ch 5, skip next ch-3 sp, sc in next ch-7 sp, ch 3, shell in next shell, ch 3, sc in next ch-7 sp, ch 5, skip next ch-3 sp, sc in next ch-7 sp,

ch 3, 3 dc in last dc, turn.

Row 10: (Ch 3, 2 dc) in first st, skip next ch-3 sp, 11 tr in next ch-5 sp, skip next ch-3 sp, shell in next shell, skip next ch-3 sp, 11 tr in next ch-5 sp, skip next ch-3 sp, 3 dc in last dc, turn. Fasten off.

Third–Fourth Lacing
Work same as Second Lacing.

Fifth Lacing
Row 1: With right side facing you, join with sl st in end of row 8 on last Scallop, (dc joining, 3 dc) in end of same row as joining sl st, ch 7, sc in end of row 4, ch 3, sc in end of row 2, ch 7, (2 dc, ch 2, 2 dc) in unworked st on Foundation (shell made), ch 7, sc in end of row 2 on other side, ch 3, sc in end of row 4, ch 7, 3 dc in end of row 8, turn. (6 dc, 6 ch sps, 1 shell made)

Rows 2–10: Work same as rows 2–10 of Second Lacing on Section A.

SECTION B
Row 1: With right side facing you, join with sc in first st on row 10 of First Lacing made, sc in next 15 sts, skip ch sp, sc in next 15 sts, (sc last st on this Lacing and first st on next Lacing tog, working across next Lacing, sc in next 15 sts, skip next ch sp, sc in next 15 sts) across, turn. (155 sc made)

Rows 2–6: Working these rows in **back lps**, ch 1, sc in each st across, turn.

SECTION C
First Lacing
Row 1: Working in **both lps**, (ch 3, 2 dc) in first st, ch 7, skip next 5 sts, sc in next st, ch 3, skip next 2 sts, sc in next st, ch 7, skip next 5 sts, (2 dc, ch 2, 2 dc) in next st (shell made), ch 7, skip next 5 sts, sc in next st, ch 3, skip next 2 sts, sc in next st, ch 7, skip next 5 sts, 3 dc in next st leaving remaining sts unworked, turn. (6 dc, 6 ch sps, 1 shell made)

Rows 2–10: Repeat rows 2–10 of First Lacing on Section A.

Second Lacing
Row 1: Working in both lps, join with sl st in next unworked st on row 6 of Section B, (dc joining, 3 dc) in first st, ch 7, skip next 5 sts, sc in next st, ch 3, skip next 2 sts, sc in next st, ch 7, skip next 5 sts, (2 dc, ch 2, 2 dc) in next st (shell made), ch 7, skip next 5 sts, sc in next st, ch 3, skip next 2 sts, sc in next st, ch 7, skip next 5 sts, 3 dc in next st leaving remaining sts unworked, turn. (6 dc, 6 ch sps, 1 shell made)

Rows 2–10: Repeat rows 2–10 of Second Lacing on Section A.

Third–Fourth Lacing
Work same as Second Lacing.

Fifth Lacing
Row 1: Working in both lps, join with sl st in next unworked st on row 6 of Section B, (dc joining, 3 dc) in first st, ch 7, skip next 5 sts, sc in next st, ch 3, skip next 2 sts, sc in next st, ch 7, skip next 5 sts, (2 dc, ch 2, 2 dc) in next st (shell made), ch 7, skip next 5 sts, sc in next st, ch 3, skip next 2 sts, sc in next st, ch 7, skip next 5 sts, 3 dc in next st, turn. (6 dc, 6 ch sps, 1 shell made)

Rows 2–10: Repeat rows 2–10 of Second Lacing on Section A.

SECTION D
Work same as Section B.

SECTION E
Work same as Section C.

SECTION F
Row 1: With right side facing you, join with sc in first st on row 10 of First Lacing made, sc in next 15 sts, skip ch sp, sc in next 15 sts, (sc last st on this Lacing and first st on next Lacing tog, working across next Lacing, sc in next 15 sts, skip next ch sp, sc in next 15 sts) across, turn. (155 sc made)

Rows 2–3: Working these rows in back lps, ch 1, sc in each st across, turn. At end of last row, fasten off.

Match and sew back lp of sts on last rows together. ❑❑

Pineapple Lace
Baby Afghan

Designed by Lisa Falk

FINISHED SIZE:
33" x 39".

MATERIALS:
❑ 7 oz. each white, pastel variegated and pink variegated
sport yarn
❑ Tapestry needle
❑ F hook or hook size needed to
obtain gauge

GAUGE:
Strip is 4" wide; rows 1-8 = 2¾".

BASIC STITCHES:
Ch, sl st, sc, hdc, dc.

SPECIAL STITCHES:
For **double cluster (dbl cl),**
*yo, insert hook in next row,
yo, draw lp through, yo, draw

through 2 lps on hook, yo, insert
hook in same row, yo, draw lp
through, yo, draw through 2 lps
on hook; repeat from *, yo, draw
through all 5 lps on hook.

For **cluster (cl),** yo, insert hook
in next row, yo, draw lp through,
yo, draw through 2 lps on hook,
yo, insert hook in same row,

yo, draw lp through, yo, draw through 2 lps on hook, yo, draw through all 3 lps on hook.

STRIP (make 5 pink variegated and 4 pastel variegated)

Row 1: Ch 12, dc in fourth ch from hook, (ch 2, skip next 2 chs, dc in next 2 chs) across, turn. *(6 dc, 2 ch sps made)*

Row 2: Ch 3 *(counts as first dc)*, dc in next st, ch 2, 3 dc in each of next 2 sts, ch 2, dc in last 2 sts, turn. *(10 dc, 2 ch sps)*

Row 3: Ch 3, dc in next st, ch 2, dc in next st, (ch 1, dc in next st) 5 times, ch 2, dc in last 2 sts, turn. *(10 dc, 7 ch sps)*

Row 4: Ch 3, dc in next st, ch 2, skip next ch sp, sc in next ch sp, (ch 3, sc in next ch sp) 4 times, ch 2, skip next ch sp, dc in last 2 sts, turn. *(6 ch sps)*

Row 5: Ch 3, dc in next st, ch 2, skip next ch sp, sc in next ch sp, (ch 3, sc in next ch sp) 3 times, ch 2, skip next ch sp, dc in last 2 sts, turn. *(5 ch sps)*

Row 6: Ch 3, dc in next st, ch 2, skip next ch sp, sc in next ch sp, (ch 3, sc in next ch sp) 2 times,

ch 2, skip next ch sp, dc in last 2 sts, turn. *(4 ch sps)*

Row 7: Ch 3, dc in next st, ch 2, skip next ch sp, sc in next ch sp, ch 3, sc in next ch sp, ch 2, skip next ch sp, dc in last 2 sts, turn. *(3 ch sps)*

Row 8: Ch 3, dc in next st, ch 2, skip next ch sp, sc in next ch sp, ch 2, skip next ch sp, dc in last 2 sts, turn.

Row 9: Ch 3, dc in next st, ch 2, 2 dc in next st, ch 2, dc in last 2 sts, turn.

Rows 10-112: Repeat rows 2-9 consecutively, ending with row 8. At end of last row, fasten off.

Edging

Row 1: Working in ends of rows across one long edge, join white with sl st in first row, (ch 2, dc) in same sp *(counts as first cl)*, ch 2, skip next row, 2 sc in each of next 4 rows, ch 2, skip next row, ***dbl cl** *(see Special Stitches)*, ch 2, skip next row, 2 sc in each of next 4 rows, ch 2, skip next row; repeat from * across to last row, **cl** *(see Special Stitches)* in last row, turn.

Row 2: Ch 2 *(counts as first hdc)*,

hdc in each st and in each ch across, turn. Fasten off.
Starting on last row, repeat on other side of Strip.

Assembly

Holding Strips wrong sides together, matching sts, working through both thicknesses in **back lps** *(see Stitch Guide)* with white, sl st together alternately, starting and ending with pink variegated Strip.

Afghan Edging

Row 1: Working across top of Afghan, with right side facing you, join white with sc in end of first row on Edging, sc in same row, 2 sc in end of next row, (*2 sc in sp between next 2 dc, ch 2, work dbl cl over next 2 ch sps, ch 2, 2 sc in sp between next 2 dc*, 2 sc in end of each of next 4 rows skipping seam in between) 8 times; repeat between **, 2 sc in end of each of last 2 rows, turn.

Row 2: Ch 2, hdc in each st across, turn. Fasten off.
Repeat on bottom edge of Afghan.❑❑

Sunset Pineapples Centerpiece

Designed by Sylvia Landman

FINISHED SIZE:
23" across.

MATERIALS:
- ❑ 284 yds. each pale gold and dk. gold size 10 crochet cotton thread
- ❑ Size 80 tatting thread:
  424 yds. shaded oranges (D)
  212 yds each shaded golds (C), shaded red/oranges (E) and gold (B)
  106 yds. shaded yellows (A)
- ❑ No. 7 steel hook or hook size needed to obtain gauge

GAUGE:
Rnds 1-5 = 2½" across.

BASIC STITCHES:
Ch, sl st, sc, hdc, dc, tr.

SPECIAL STITCHES:
For **shell**, (2 dc, ch 3, 2 dc) in next ch sp.

For **beginning shell (beg shell),** ch 3, (dc, ch 3, 2 dc) in same sp.

For **beginning double shell (beg dbl shell),** ch 3, (dc, ch 3, 2 dc, ch 3, 2 dc) in same sp.

For **double shell (dbl shell),** (2 dc, ch 3, 2 dc, ch 3, 2 dc) in next shell.

For **picot,** ch 3, sl st in third ch from hook.

NOTE:
To create shading effects, varie-gated tatting threads are used in combination with crochet cotton. Working with multiple threads enables you to change one strand at a time creating subtle coloration changes. Work throughout with one strand of crochet cotton and two strands tatting thread held together as one.

CENTERPIECE
Rnd 1: With pale gold crochet cotton and one strand each A and B tatting thread, ch 8, sl st in first ch to form ring, ch 1, 12 sc in ring, join with sl st in first sc. *(12 sc made)*

Rnd 2: Ch 1, sc in first st, (ch 3, sc in next st) around; to **join,** ch 1, hdc in first sc *(counts as ch sp).*

Rnd 3: Ch 1, sc around joining hdc, (ch 4, sc in next ch sp) around; to **join,** ch 2, hdc in first sc.

Rnd 4: Ch 1, sc around joining hdc, (ch 5, sc in next ch sp) around; to **join,** ch 2, dc in first sc.

Rnd 5: Ch 1, sc around joining dc, (ch 6, sc in next ch sp) around; to **join,** ch 3, dc in first sc.

Rnd 6: Ch 1, sc around joining dc, ch 7, (sc in next ch sp, ch 7) around, join with sl st in first sc.

Rnd 7: Ch 1, sc in first st, ch 2, **shell** *(see Special Stitches)* in next ch sp, ch 2, (sc in next st, ch 2, shell in next ch sp, ch 2) around, join. *(12 shells, 12 sc)* Fasten off A and add a second strand of B.

Rnds 8-9: Ch 6 *(counts as first dc and ch-3 sp),* shell in ch sp of next shell, ch 3, (dc in next st, ch 3, shell in ch sp of next shell, ch 3) around, join with sl st in third ch of ch-6.

Rnd 10: (Ch 5, dc) in first st, ch 3, shell in next shell, ch 3, *(dc, ch 2, dc) in next st, ch 3, shell in next shell, ch 3; repeat from * around, join with sl st in third ch of ch-6. Fasten off one strand of B and add one strand of C.

Rnd 11: Sl st in first ch sp, **beg shell** (see Special Stitches), ch 3, skip next ch sp, (shell in next shell or in next ch sp, ch 3, skip next ch sp) around, join with sl st in top of ch-3. (24 shells)

Rnds 12-13: Sl st in next st, sl st in next ch sp, beg shell, ch 3, skip next ch sp, (shell in next shell, ch 3, skip next ch sp) around, join.

Rnd 14: Sl st in next st, sl st in next ch sp, beg shell, ch 3, skip next ch sp, (2 dc, ch 5, 2 dc) in next shell, ch 3, skip next ch sp, *shell in next shell, ch 3, skip next ch sp, (2 dc, ch 5, 2 dc) in next shell, ch 3, skip next ch sp; repeat from * around, join.

Rnd 15: Sl st in next st, sl st in next ch sp, beg shell, ch 3, skip next ch sp, 10 tr in next ch sp, ch 3, skip next ch sp, (shell in next shell, ch 3, skip next ch sp, 10 tr in next ch sp, ch 3, skip next ch sp) around, join.

Rnd 16: Sl st in next st, sl st in next ch sp, beg shell, ch 3, tr in next tr, (ch 1, tr in next tr) 9 times, ch 3, skip next ch sp, *shell in next shell, ch 3, tr in next tr, (ch 1, tr in next tr) 9 times, ch 3, skip next ch sp; repeat from * around, join.

Rnd 17: Sl st in next st, sl st in next ch sp, beg shell, *[ch 3, skip next ch sp, sc in next ch-1 sp, (ch 3, sc in next ch sp) 8 times, ch 3, skip next ch sp], shell in next shell; repeat from * 10 more times; repeat between [ ], join.

Rnd 18: Sl st in next st, sl st in next ch sp, beg shell, *[ch 3, skip next ch sp, sc in next ch sp, (ch 3, sc in next ch sp) 7 times, ch 3, skip next ch sp], shell in next shell; repeat from * 10 more times; repeat between [ ], join. Fasten off B and add a second strand of C.

Rnd 19: Sl st in next st, sl st in next ch sp, beg shell, *[ch 3, skip next ch sp, sc in next ch sp, (ch 3, sc in next ch sp) 6 times, ch 3, skip next ch sp], shell in next shell; repeat from * 10 more times; repeat between [ ], join.

Rnd 20: Sl st in next st, sl st in next ch sp, **beg dbl shell** (see Special Stitches), *[ch 3, skip next ch sp, sc in next ch sp, (ch 3, sc in next ch sp) 5 times, ch 3, skip next ch sp], **dbl shell** (see Special Stitches) in next shell; repeat from * 10 more times; repeat between [ ], join.

Rnd 21: Sl st in next st, sl st in next ch sp, beg shell, *[ch 3, shell in next ch sp, ch 3, skip next ch sp, sc in next ch sp, (ch 3, sc in next ch sp) 4 times, ch 3, skip next ch sp], shell in first ch sp of next dbl shell; repeat from * 10 more times; repeat between [ ], join.

Rnd 22: Sl st in next st, sl st in next ch sp, beg shell, *[(ch 3, shell in next ch sp or in next shell) 2 times, ch 3, skip next ch sp, sc in next ch sp, (ch 3, sc in next ch sp) 3 times, ch 3, skip next ch sp], shell in next shell; repeat from * 10 more times; repeat between [ ], join. Fasten off pale gold crochet cotton and add dk. gold crochet cotton.

Rnd 23: Sl st in next st, sl st in next ch sp, beg shell, *[(ch 3, shell in next shell) 2 times, ch 3, skip next ch sp, sc in next ch sp, (ch 3, sc in next ch sp) 2 times, ch 3, skip next ch sp], shell in next shell; repeat from * 10 more times; repeat between [ ], join.

Rnd 24: Sl st in next st, sl st in next ch sp, beg shell, *[ch 3, skip next ch sp, (2 dc, ch 5, 2 dc) in next shell, ch 3, skip next ch sp, shell in next shell, ch 3, skip next ch sp, (sc in next ch sp, ch 3) 2 times, skip next ch sp], shell in next shell; repeat from * 10 more times; repeat between [ ], join.

Rnd 25: Sl st in next st, sl st in next ch sp, beg shell, *[ch 4, skip next ch sp, 11 tr in next ch sp, ch 4, skip next ch sp, shell in next ch sp, ch 4, skip next ch sp, sc in next ch sp, ch 4, skip next ch sp], shell in next ch sp; repeat from * 10 more times; repeat between [ ], join. Fasten off one strand of C and add one strand of D.

Rnd 26: Sl st in next st, sl st in next ch sp, beg shell, *[ch 4, tr in next tr, (ch 1, tr in next tr) 10 times, ch 4, skip next ch sp, shell in next shell, ch 3, (2 dc in next ch sp, ch 3) 2 times], shell in next shell; repeat from * 10 more times; repeat between [ ], join.

Rnd 27: Sl st in next st, sl st in next ch sp, beg shell, *[ch 4, skip next ch sp, sc in next ch sp, (ch 3, sc in next ch sp) 9 times, ch 4, skip next ch sp, shell in next shell, ch 3, skip next ch sp, 2 dc in next ch sp, ch 3, skip next ch sp], shell in next shell; repeat from * 10 more times; repeat between [ ], join.

Rnd 28: Sl st in next st, sl st in next ch sp, beg shell, *[ch 4, skip next ch sp, sc in next ch sp, (ch 3, sc in next ch sp) 8 times, ch 4, skip next ch sp, shell in next shell, ch 3, skip next ch sp, 2 dc in next dc, ch 3, 2 dc in next dc, ch 3, skip next ch sp], shell in next shell; repeat from * 10 more times; repeat between [ ], join. Fasten off C and add a second strand of D.

Rnd 29: Sl st in next st, sl st in next ch sp, beg shell, *[ch 4, skip next ch sp, sc in next ch sp, (ch 3, sc in next ch sp) 7 times, ch 4, skip next ch sp, shell in next shell, ch 3, skip next ch sp, shell in next ch sp, ch 3, skip next ch sp], shell in next shell; repeat from * 10 more times; repeat between [ ], join.

Rnd 30: Sl st in next st, sl st in next ch sp, beg shell, ch 3, skip next ch sp, *[sc in next ch sp, (ch 3, sc in next ch sp) 6 times, ch 3, skip next ch sp], (shell in next shell, ch 3, skip next ch sp) 3 times; repeat from * 10 more times; repeat between [ ], (shell in next shell, ch 3, skip next ch sp) 2 times, join.

Rnd 31: Sl st in next st, sl st in next ch sp, beg shell, ch 3, skip next ch sp, *[sc in next ch sp, (ch 3, sc in next ch sp) 5 times, ch 3, skip next ch sp], (shell in next shell, ch 3, skip next ch sp) 3 times; repeat from * 10 more times; repeat between [ ], (shell in next shell, ch 3, skip next ch sp) 2 times, join.

Rnd 32: Sl st in next st, sl st in next ch sp, beg shell, ch 3, skip next ch sp, *[sc in next ch sp, (ch 3, sc in next ch sp) 4 times, ch 3, skip next ch sp], (shell in next shell, ch 3, skip next ch sp) 3 times; repeat from * 10 more times; repeat between [ ], (shell in next shell, ch 3, skip next ch sp) 2 times, join.

Rnd 33: Sl st in next st, sl st in next ch sp, beg shell, ch 4, skip next ch sp, *[sc in next ch sp, (ch 3, sc in next ch sp) 3 times, ch 4, skip next ch sp], (shell in next shell, ch 4, skip next ch sp) 3 times; repeat from * 10 more times; repeat between [ ], (shell in next shell, ch 4, skip next ch sp) 2 times, join. Fasten off one strand of D and add one strand of E.

Rnd 34: Sl st in next st, sl st in next ch sp, beg shell, *[ch 4, skip next ch sp, sc in next ch sp, (ch 3, sc in next ch sp) 2 times, ch 4, skip next ch sp, (shell in next shell, ch 4, sc in next ch sp, ch 4) 2 times], shell in next shell; repeat from * 10 more times; repeat between [ ], join.

Rnd 35: Sl st in next st, sl st in next ch sp, beg shell, ◊[ch 4, skip next ch sp, sc in next ch sp, ch 3, sc in next ch sp, ch 4, skip next ch sp, *shell in next shell, ch 3, (sc in next ch sp, ch 3) 2 times; repeat from *◊, shell in next shell]; repeat between [ ] 10 more times; repeat between ◊◊, join. Fasten off one strand of D and add a second strand of E.

Rnd 36: Sl st in next st, sl st in next ch sp, beg shell, ◊[ch 6, skip next ch sp, sc in next ch sp, ch 6, skip next ch sp, *shell in next shell, ch 4, (sc in next ch sp, ch 4) 3 times; repeat from *◊, shell in next shell]; repeat between [ ] 10 more times; repeat between ◊◊, join.

Rnd 37: Ch 1, sc in first 2 sts, ◊[(sc, **picot**—*see Special Stitches*, sc) in next ch sp, sc in next 2 sts, 3 sc in each of next 2 ch sps, *sc in next 2 sts, (sc, picot, sc) in next ch sp, sc in next 2 sts, 3 sc in each of next 4 ch sps; repeat from *◊, sc in next 2 sts]; repeat between [ ] 10 more times; repeat between ◊◊, join. Fasten off.❑❑

Daisy Table Runner

Designed by Janie Herrin

FINISHED SIZE:
20" x 32".

MATERIALS:
- ❑ Size 10 crochet cotton thread:
    1,050 yds. white
    350 yds. green
    350 yds. yellow
- ❑ Optional fabric glue
- ❑ No. 7 steel crochet hook or hook size needed to obtain gauge

GAUGE:
Rnds 1-4 = 2¾" across. Each Motif is 6" across.

OPTIONAL:
As an alternative method for weaving in thread ends, cut thread leaving a 4" end, thread through tapestry needle. Coat thread with glue approximately 1" from last st made, weave end through sts for about 1". Trim excess and let dry.

FIRST ROW
First Motif
Rnd 1: With yellow, ch 6, sl st in first ch to form ring, ch 1, (sc in

ring, ch 20) 12 times, join with sl st in first sc. Fasten off. *(12 ch lps made)*

Rnd 2: Being careful not to twist loops, join green with sc in any ch lp, 2 sc in same lp, ch 5, (3 sc in next ch lp, ch 5) around, join. *(36 sc, 12 ch sps)*

Rnd 3: Sl st in next st, ch 1, sc in same st, ch 5, sc in next ch sp, ch 5, (sc in 2nd st of next 3-sc group, ch 5, sc in next ch sp, ch 5) around, join. *(24 ch sps)*

Rnd 4: Sl st in first ch sp, ch 4, (3 tr, ch 5, 4 tr) in same sp, ch 5, skip next ch sp, (sc in next ch sp, ch 5) 3 times, skip next ch sp, *(4 tr, ch 5, 4 tr) in next ch sp, ch 5, skip next ch sp, (sc in next ch sp, ch 5) 3 times, skip next ch sp; repeat from * around, join with sl st in top of ch-4. Fasten off. *(32 tr, 20 ch sps)*

Rnd 5: Join white with sl st in first st, ch 3, dc in next 3 sts, *[ch 5, dc in next ch sp, ch 5, dc in next 4 sts, ch 5, (sc in next ch sp, ch 5) 4 times], dc in next 4 sts; repeat from * 2 more times; repeat between [ ], join with sl st in top of ch-3.

Rnd 6: Ch 3, dc in next 3 sts, *[ch 5, (dc in next ch sp, ch 5) 2 times, dc in next 4 sts, ch 5, skip next ch sp, (sc in next ch sp, ch 5) 3 times, skip next ch sp], dc in next 4 sts; repeat from * 2 more times; repeat between [ ], join.

Rnd 7: Ch 3, dc in next 3 sts, *[ch 5, dc in next ch sp, ch 5, (dc, ch 5, dc) in next ch sp, ch 5, dc in next ch sp, ch 5, dc in next 4 sts, ch 5, skip next ch sp, (sc in next ch sp, ch 5) 2 times, skip next ch sp], dc in next 4 sts; repeat from * 2 more times; repeat between [ ], join.

Rnd 8: Ch 3, dc in next 3 sts, *[ch 5, (dc in next ch sp, ch 5) 2 times, (3 dc, ch 5, 3 dc) in next ch sp, ch 5, (dc in next ch sp, ch 5) 2 times, dc in next 4 sts, ch 5, skip next ch sp, sc in next ch sp, ch 5, skip next ch sp], dc in next 4 sts; repeat from * 2 more times; repeat between [ ], join.

Rnd 9: Ch 3, dc in next 3 sts, *[4 dc in next ch sp, (dc in next st, 4 dc in next ch sp) 2 times, ch 3, (dc, ch 5, dc) in next ch sp, ch 3, 4 dc in next ch sp, (dc in next st, 4 dc in next ch sp) 2 times, dc in next 4 sts, ch 5, skip next 2 ch sps], dc in next 4 sts; repeat from * 2 more times; repeat between [ ], join.

Rnd 10: Ch 3, dc in next 3 sts, *[ch 7, skip next 4 sts, (sc in next st, ch 7, skip next 4 sts) 2 times, sc in next ch sp, ch 7, (dc, ch 7, dc) in next ch sp, ch 7, sc in next ch sp, ch 7, skip next 4 sts, (sc in next st, ch 7, skip next 4 sts) 2 times, dc in next 4 sts, sc in next ch sp], dc in next 4 sts; repeat from * 2 more times; repeat between [ ], join. *(8 ch sps across each side between corner ch sps)*

Second Motif

Rnds 1-9: Repeat same rnds of First Motif.

Note: *For **joining ch sp**, ch 3, sc in corresponding ch sp on other Motif, ch 3.*

Rnd 10: Ch 3, dc in next 3 sts, ch 7, skip next 4 sts, (sc in next st, ch 7, skip next 4 sts) 2 times, sc in next ch sp, ch 7, dc in next ch sp; joining to side of last Motif, work joining ch sp, dc in same sp on this Motif, work joining ch sp, sc in next ch sp on this Motif, work joining ch sp, skip next 4 sts on this Motif, (sc in next st, work joining ch sp, skip next 4 sts on this Motif) 2 times, dc in next 4 sts, sc in next ch sp, dc in next 4 sts, work joining ch sp, skip next 4 sts on this Motif, (sc in next st, work joining ch sp, skip next 4 sts on this Motif) 2 times, sc in next ch sp, work joining ch sp, dc in next ch sp on this Motif, work joining ch sp, dc in same sp on this Motif, *[ch 7, sc in next ch sp, ch 7, skip next 4 sts, (sc in next st, ch 7, skip next 4 sts) 2 times, dc in next 4 sts, sc in next ch sp], dc in next 4 sts, ch 7, skip next 4 sts, (sc in next st, ch 7, skip next 4 sts) 2 times, sc in next ch sp, ch 7, (dc, ch 7, dc) in next ch sp; repeat from*; repeat between [ ], join. Fasten off.

Repeat Second Motif one more time for a total of 3 Motifs on this row.

SECOND ROW
First Motif

Joining to bottom of First Motif on last row, work same as First Row Second Motif.

Second Motif

Rnds 1-9: Repeat same rnds of First Row First Motif.

Rnd 10: Ch 3, dc in next 3 sts, ch 7, skip next 4 sts, (sc in next st, ch 7, skip next 4 sts) 2 times, sc in next ch sp, ch 7, dc in next ch sp; joining to bottom of next Motif on last row, work joining ch sp, dc in same sp on this Motif, *work joining ch sp, sc in next ch sp on this Motif, work joining ch sp, skip next 4 sts on this Motif, (sc in next st, work joining ch sp, skip next 4 sts on this Motif) 2 times, dc in next 4 sts, sc in next ch sp, dc in next 4 sts, work joining ch sp, skip next 4 sts on this Motif, (sc in next st, work joining ch sp, skip next 4 sts on this Motif) 2 times, sc in next ch sp, work joining ch sp, dc in next ch sp on this Motif, work joining ch sp, dc in same sp on this Motif*; joining to side of last Motif on this row; repeat between **, [ch 7, sc in next ch sp, ch 7, skip next 4 sts, (sc in next st, ch 7, skip next 4 sts) 2 times, dc in next 4 sts, sc in next ch sp], dc in next 4 sts, ch 7, skip next 4 sts, (sc in next st, ch 7, skip next 4 sts) 2 times, sc in next ch sp, ch 7, (dc, ch 7, dc) in next ch sp; repeat between [ ], join. Fasten off.

Repeat Second Motif one more time for a total of 3 Motifs on this row.

Repeat Second Row 3 more times for a total of 5 rows.

Border

Notes: *For **beginning shell (beg shell)**, ch 5, tr in same sp, (ch 1, tr in same sp) 5 times.*

*For **shell**, tr in next ch sp, (ch 1, tr in same sp) 6 times.*

Rnd 1: Working around entire outer edge, join white with sl st in corner ch sp before one short end, beg shell, ◊*[(ch 1, sc in next ch sp, ch 1, shell in next ch sp) 2 times, ch 1, sc in next sc between 4-dc groups, ch 1, (shell in next ch sp, ch 1, sc in next ch sp, ch 1) 2 times], (tr, ch 1, tr, ch 1, tr) in next joining ch sp, ch 1, tr around side of next joining sc, ch 1, (tr, ch 1, tr, ch 1, tr) in next joining ch sp (last 7 tr made count as one shell)*; repeat between **; repeat between [ ]; shell in next corner ch sp; repeat between ** 4 more times; repeat between [ ]◊, shell in next corner ch sp; repeat between ◊◊, join with sl st in 4th ch of ch-5. *(14 shells across each short end between corner shells, 24 shells across each long edge between corner shells)*

Rnd 2: Sl st in next ch sp, ch 3, dc in same sp, 2 dc in each of next 5 ch sps, ch 1, sc in next sc, ch 1, (2 dc in each of next 6 ch sps, ch 1, sc in next sc, ch 1) around, join with sl st in top of ch-3. Fasten off.

Rnd 3: Ch 2, dc next 2 sts tog, (ch 4, dc next 3 sts tog) 3 times, ch 2, sc next 2 ch sps tog, ch 2, *dc next 3 sts tog, (ch 4, dc next 3 sts tog) 3 times, ch 2, sc next 2 ch sps tog, ch 2; repeat from * around, join with sl st in top of first st. Fasten off.◻◻

Square Pineapple Doily

Designed by Janie Herrin

FINISHED SIZE:
8½" across.

MATERIALS:
❑ 350 yds. pink size 10 crochet cotton

❑ No. 7 steel crochet hook or hook size needed to obtain gauge

GAUGE:
Rnds 1-5 = 2¼" across.

DOILY

Rnd 1: Ch 4, 15 dc in fourth ch from hook, join with sl st in top of ch-3. *(16 dc)*

Rnd 2: Ch 1, sc in first st, ch 3, skip next st, (sc in next st, ch 3, skip next st) around, join with sl st in first sc. *(8 sc, 8 ch sps)*

Rnd 3: Sl st in next ch sp, ch 3, 4 dc in same sp, 5 dc in each ch sp around, join with sl st in top of ch-3. *(40 dc)*

Rnd 4: Ch 1, sc in first st, ch 3, skip next st, (sc in next st, ch 3, skip next st) around, join with sl st in first sc. *(20 sc, 20 ch sps)*

Rnd 5: Sl st in next ch, ch 1, sc in same sp, ch 4, (sc in next ch sp, ch 4) around, join.

Rnd 6: Sl st in each of next 2 chs, ch 1, sc in same sp, ch 4, (sc in next ch sp, ch 4) around, join.

Rnd 7: Sl st in each of next 2 chs, ch 1, sc in same sp, (ch 5, sc in next ch sp) 2 times, 7 dc in next ch sp, sc in next ch sp, *(ch 5, sc in next ch sp) 3 times, 7 dc in next ch sp, sc in next ch sp; repeat from * 2 more times, ch 5, join. *(28 dc, 12 ch sps)*

Rnd 8: Sl st in next ch sp, ch 5, tr in same sp, (ch 1, tr in same sp) 5 times, *[ch 1, sc in next ch sp, ch 1, tr in next sc, (ch 1, tr in next dc) 7 times, ch 1, tr in next sc, ch 1, sc in next ch sp, ch 1], tr in next ch sp, (ch 1, tr in same sp) 6 times; repeat from * 2 more times; repeat between [ ], join with sl st in 4th ch of ch-5.

Rnd 9: Ch 5, dc in next tr, (ch 2, dc in next tr) 5 times, *[ch 2, sc in next sc, ch 2, sc in next tr, (ch 2, sc in next tr) 8 times, ch 2, sc in next sc, ch 2], dc in next tr, (ch 2, dc in next tr) 6 times; repeat from * 2 more times; repeat between [ ], join with sl st in 3rd ch of ch-5.

Rnd 10: Sl st in next ch sp, ch 3, dc in same sp, *[(ch 2, 2 dc in next ch sp) 5 times, ch 2, sc in next sc, ch 2, skip next ch sp, sc in next ch sp, (ch 2, sc in next ch sp) 7 times, ch 2, sc in next sc, ch 2, skip next ch sp], 2 dc in next ch sp; repeat from * 2 more times; repeat between [ ], join with sl st in top of ch-3.

Rnd 11: Sl st in next st, sl st in next ch sp, ch 3, 3 dc in same sp, 4 dc in next ch sp, *[5 dc in next ch sp, 4 dc in each of next 2 ch sps, ch 3, skip next 2 ch sps, sc in next ch sp, (ch 3, sc in next ch sp) 6 times, ch 3, skip next 2 ch sps], 4 dc in each of next 2 ch sps; repeat from * 2 more times; repeat between [ ], join.

Rnd 12: Ch 5, skip next st, dc in next st, (ch 2, skip next st, dc in next st) 9 times, *[ch 3, skip next ch sp, sc in next ch sp, (ch 3, sc in next ch sp) 5 times, ch 3, skip next ch sp], dc in next st,

(ch 2, skip next st, dc in next st) 10 times; repeat from * 2 more times; repeat between [ ], join with sl st in 3rd ch of ch-5.

Rnd 13: Sl st in next ch sp, ch 3, 2 dc in same sp, 3 dc in each of next 9 ch sps, *[ch 3, skip next ch sp, sc in next ch sp, (ch 3, sc in next ch sp) 4 times, ch 3, skip next ch sp], 3 dc in each of next 10 ch sps; repeat from * 2 more times; repeat between [ ], join with sl st in top of ch-3.

Rnd 14: Ch 5, skip next st, (dc in next st, ch 2, skip next st) 5 times, *[dc in next 3 sts, ch 5, dc in next 3 sts, (ch 2, skip next st, dc in next st) 6 times, ch 3, skip next ch sp, sc in next ch sp, (ch 3, sc in next ch sp) 3 times, ch 3, skip next ch sp], (dc in next st, ch 2, skip next st) 6 times; repeat from * 2 more times; repeat between [ ], join with sl st in third ch of ch-5.

Rnd 15: Sl st in next ch sp, ch 3, 2 dc in same sp, 3 dc in each of next 5 ch sps, *[ch 2, (3 dc, ch 5, 3 dc) in next ch sp, ch 2, 3 dc in each of next 6 ch sps, ch 3, skip next ch sp, sc in next ch sp, (ch 3, sc in next ch sp) 2 times, ch 3, skip next ch sp], 3 dc in each of next 6 ch sps; repeat from * 2 more times; repeat between [ ], join with sl st in top of ch-3.

Rnd 16: Ch 1, sc in first st, ch 3, skip next 2 sts, (sc in next st, ch 3, skip next 2 sts) 5 times, *[dc

in next ch sp, ch 3, (3 dc, ch 5, 3 dc) in next ch sp, ch 3, dc in next ch sp, (ch 3, skip next 2 sts, sc in next st) 6 times, ch 3, skip next ch sp, (sc in next ch sp, ch 3) 2 times, skip next ch sp], (sc in next st, ch 3, skip next 2 sts) 6 times; repeat from * 2 more times; repeat between [ ], join with sl st in first sc.

Rnd 17: Sl st in next ch sp, ch 1, sc in same sp, ch 4, (sc in next ch sp, ch 4) 6 times, *[(sc, ch 4, sc) in next ch sp, (ch 4, sc in next ch sp) 7 times, ch 3, skip next ch sp, sc in next ch sp, ch 3, skip next ch sp], (sc in next ch sp, ch 4) 7 times; repeat from * 2 more times; repeat between [ ], join.

Rnd 18: Sl st in next ch sp, ch 1, sc in same sp, ch 4, (sc in next ch sp, ch 4) 6 times, (sc, ch 4, sc) in next ch sp, ch 4, *(sc in next ch sp, ch 4) 16 times, (sc, ch 4, sc) in next ch sp, ch 4; repeat from * 2 more times, (sc in next ch sp, ch 4) 9 times, join.

Rnd 19: Ch 1, sc in first st, ch 1, skip next ch sp, tr in next ch sp, (ch 1, tr in same sp) 6 times, ch 1, skip next ch sp, *sc in next st, ch 1, skip next ch sp, tr in next ch sp, (ch 1, tr in same sp) 6 times, ch 1, skip next ch sp; repeat from * around, join.

Rnd 20: Ch 1, sc in first st, ch 3, (sc in next st, ch 3) around, join. Fasten off.❏❏

Pillow Edging

Designed by Josie Rabier

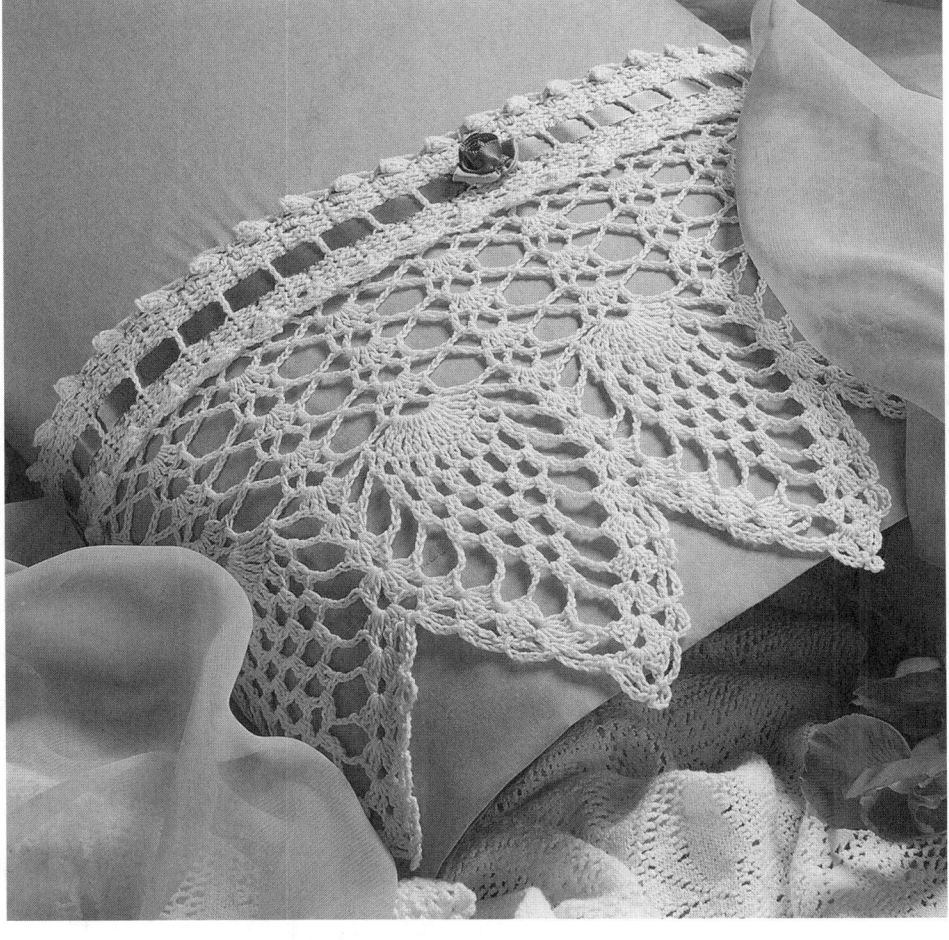

FINISHED SIZE:
9" wide. Fits standard pillowcase.

MATERIALS FOR ONE:
- ❑ 650 yds. ecru size 10 crochet cotton
- ❑ 40" purple ⅜" satin picot ribbon
- ❑ One purple ⅝" satin ribbon rose with leaves
- ❑ Purple sewing thread
- ❑ Sewing needle
- ❑ No. 7 steel hook or hook size needed to obtain gauge

GAUGE:
8 dc and one ch-3 sp = 1⅜"; 3 dc rows = 1".

TOP

Row 1: Ch 13, dc in fourth ch from hook, dc in next 2 chs, ch 3, skip next 3 chs, dc in last 4 chs, turn. *(8 dc, 1 ch-3 sp made)*

Rows 2-112: Ch 3, dc in next 3 sts, ch 3, skip next ch sp, dc in last 4 sts, turn. At end of last row, matching sts and working through both thicknesses, sl st first row to last row. **Do not fasten off.**

Pineapple

Rnd 1: Working in ends of rows, ch 2, hdc in first row, 2 hdc in each row around, join with sl st in top of ch-2. *(224 hdc made)*

Rnd 2: Ch 3, skip next 2 sts, dc in next st, ch 5, (dc in next st, skip next 2 sts, dc in next st, ch 5) around, join with sl st in top of ch-3. *(56 ch sps)*

Rnd 3: Sl st in next st, sl st in next ch sp, ch 3, 4 dc in same sp, ch 3, sl st in center st of next ch sp, ch 3, (5 dc in next ch sp, ch 3, sl st in center st of next ch sp, ch 3) around, join. *(140 dc, 56 ch sps)*

Rnd 4: Ch 3, *[skip next st, (dc, ch 5, dc) in next st, skip next st, dc in next st, ch 5, skip next 2 ch sps], dc in next st; repeat from * around to last 4 sts and 2 ch sps; repeat between [ ], join.

Rnd 5: Sl st in next st, sl st in next ch sp, ch 3, 4 dc in same sp, ch 3, sl st in center ch of next ch sp, ch 3, (5 dc in next ch sp, ch 3, sl st in center ch of next ch sp, ch 3) around, join.

Rnds 6-8: Repeat rnds 4 and 5 alternately, ending with rnd 4.

Notes: *For **beginning shell (beg shell),** ch 3, (2 dc, ch 3, 3 dc) in same sp.*
*For **shell,** (3 dc, ch 3, 3 dc) in next ch sp.*

Rnd 9: Sl st in next st, sl st in next ch sp, beg shell, *[ch 3, sl st in center ch of next ch sp, 14 tr in next ch sp, sl st in center ch of next ch sp, ch 3], shell in next ch sp; repeat from * 12 more times; repeat between [ ], join.

Rnd 10: Sl st in next 2 sts, sl st in next ch sp, beg shell, *[ch 3, skip next ch sp, dc in next 2 tr, (ch 2, dc in next 2 tr) 6 times, ch 3, skip next ch sp], shell in ch sp of next shell; repeat from * 12 more times; repeat between [ ], join.

Rnd 11: Sl st in next 2 sts, sl st in next ch sp, beg shell, *[ch 3, skip next ch sp, 2 dc in next ch sp, (ch 2, 2 dc in next ch sp) 5 times, ch 3, skip next ch sp], shell in next shell; repeat from * 12 more times; repeat between [ ], join.

Notes: *For **beginning double shell (beg dbl shell),** ch 3, (2 dc, ch 3, 3 dc, ch 3, 3 dc) in same sp.*
*For **double shell (dbl shell),** (3 dc, ch 3, 3 dc, ch 3, 3 dc) in next ch sp.*

Rnd 12: Sl st in next 2 sts, sl st in next ch sp, beg dbl shell, *[ch 3, skip next ch sp, 2 dc in next ch sp, (ch 2, 2 dc in next ch sp) 4 times, ch 3, skip next ch sp], dbl shell in next shell; repeat from *

12 more times; repeat between [ ], join.

Rnd 13: Sl st in next 2 sts, sl st in next ch sp, beg shell, shell in next ch sp, *[ch 3, skip next ch sp, 2 dc in next ch sp, (ch 2, 2 dc in next ch sp) 3 times, ch 3, skip next ch sp], shell in each of next 2 ch sps; repeat from * 12 more times; repeat between [ ], join.

Row 14: For **first pineapple,** working in rows, sl st in next 2 sts, sl st in next 3 chs, sl st in next 4 sts, ch 4, shell in next shell, ch 3, skip next ch sp, 2 dc in next ch sp, (ch 2, 2 dc in next ch sp) 2 times, ch 3, skip next ch sp, shell in next shell, tr in last st of same shell leaving remaining sts unworked, turn. *(2 shells, 2 tr, 2 ch-3 sps, 2 ch-2 sps)*

Row 15: Ch 4, shell in next shell, ch 3, skip next ch sp, 2 dc in next ch sp, ch 2, 2 dc in next ch sp, ch 3, skip next ch sp, shell in next shell, tr in top of last ch-4, turn.

Row 16: Ch 4, shell in next shell, ch 3, skip next ch sp, 2 dc in next ch sp, ch 3, skip next ch sp, shell in next shell, tr in top of last ch-4, turn.

Row 17: Ch 4, shell in next shell,

skip next 2 ch sps, sl st in next shell, ch 4, sl st in top of ch-4, turn.

Row 18: Ch 4, skip next ch sp, shell in next shell, sl st in last st of same shell, **do not turn.** Fasten off.

Row 14: For **next pineapple,** working in rows, join with sl st in first st of next shell on rnd 13, ch 4, shell in next shell, ch 3, skip next ch sp, 2 dc in next ch sp, (ch 2, 2 dc in next ch sp) 2 times, ch 3, skip next ch sp, shell in next shell, tr in last st of same shell leaving remaining sts unworked, turn.

Rows 15-18: Repeat same rows of first pineapple.

Repeat next pineapple 12 more times for a total of 14 pineapples. At end of last pineapple, **do not fasten off.**

Rnd 19: Working in ends of rows around pineapples, ch 5, (sl st in top of next row, ch 5) 3 times, *[sl st in last st of next shell on rnd 13, sl st in first st of next shell, ch 5, (sl st in top of next row, ch 5) 4 times, (sl st, ch 5, sl st) in ch sp of next shell, ch 5], (sl st in top of next row, ch 5) 4 times; repeat from * 12 more

times; repeat between [ ], join with sl st in last sl st on row 18 of last pineapple. Fasten off.

Edging
Note: *For **popcorn (pc),** 5 dc in next st, drop lp from hook, insert hook in first st of 5-dc group, draw dropped lp through.*

Working in skipped sts of rnd 1 on Pineapple, with Top facing you, join with sl st in first skipped st, ch 5, pc in next st, ch 1, (sl st in next skipped st, ch 5, pc in next st, ch 1) around, join with sl st in first sl st. Fasten off.

TOP EDGING
Rnd 1: Working in ends of rows around opposite side of Top, join with sl st in any row, ch 2, hdc in same row, 2 hdc in each row around, join with sl st in top of ch-2.

Rnd 2: Ch 5, pc in next st, ch 1, skip next 2 sts, (sl st in next st, ch 5, pc in next st, ch 1, skip next 2 sts) around, join with sl st in first ch of first ch-5. Fasten off.

Weave ribbon through ch sps in center of Top; secure ends. Sew ribbon rose to ribbon.❑❑

Lace Jacket

Designed by Shirley Patterson

FINISHED SIZES & GAUGES:
For **small/medium,** using No. 5 steel crochet hook, each Strip is 2¼" wide (3" wide after joining); one pattern repeat (rows 3-9 of Strip) = 2½".

For **large/extra large,** using No. 3 steel crochet hook, each Strip is 2½" wide (3¼" wide after joining); one pattern repeat (rows 3-9) = 3".

MATERIALS:
- ❑ Size 10 crochet cotton thread: 1500 yds.for small/medium 2000 yds. for large/extra large
- ❑ 1 yd. of ¼" satin ribbon
- ❑ Tapestry needle
- ❑ Steel hook needed to obtain size and gauge given above

NOTE:
Bed Jacket is made in strips from shoulder to shoulder.

FIRST STRIP
Row 1: For **first half of Strip,** starting at shoulder, ch 18, sc in second ch from hook, sc in each ch across, turn. *(17 sc made)*
Note: For **shell,** *(2 dc, ch 2, 2 dc) in next st or ch sp.*
Row 2: Ch 3, skip next 2 sts, shell in next st, ch 1, skip next 4 sts, (dc, ch 3, dc) in next st, ch 1, skip next 4 sts, shell in next st, skip next 2 sts, dc in last st, turn. *(4 dc, 2 shells, 2 ch-1 sps, 1 ch-3 sp)*
Row 3: Ch 3, shell in ch sp of next shell, ch 1, skip next ch sp, 5 tr in next ch sp, ch 1, skip next ch sp, shell in ch sp of next shell, dc in last dc, turn.

Row 4: Ch 3, shell in next shell, dc in next tr, (ch 1, dc in next tr) 4 times, shell in next shell, dc in last st, turn.
Row 5: Ch 3, shell in next shell, ch 1, sc in next ch sp, (ch 3, sc in next ch sp) 3 times, ch 1, shell in next shell, dc in last dc, turn.
Row 6: Ch 3, shell in next shell, ch 2, skip next ch sp, sc in next ch sp, (ch 3, sc in next ch sp) 2 times, ch 2, skip next ch sp, shell in next shell, dc in last st, turn.
Row 7: Ch 3, shell in next shell, ch 3, skip next ch sp, (sc in next ch sp, ch 3) 2 times, shell in next shell, dc in last st, turn.
Row 8: Ch 3, shell in next shell, ch 4, skip next ch sp, sc in next ch sp, ch 4, shell in next shell, dc in last st, turn.
Row 9: Ch 3, shell in next shell, ch 3, skip next ch sp, (dc, ch 3, dc) in next st, ch 3, skip next ch sp, shell in next shell, dc in last dc, turn.
Rows 10-50: Repeat rows 3-9 consecutively, ending with row 8. At end of last row, fasten off.
Row 51: For **second half of Strip;** working in starting ch on opposite side of row 1, join with sl st in first ch, ch 3, skip next 2 chs, shell in next ch, ch 1, skip next 4 chs, (dc, ch 3, dc) in next ch, ch 1, skip next 4 chs, shell in next ch, skip next 2 chs, dc in last ch, turn. *(4 dc, 2 shells, 2 ch-1 sps, 1 ch-3 sp)*
Rows 52-99: Repeat rows 3-9 of first half of Strip consecutively, ending with row 8. At end of last row, do not turn or fasten off.
For **first side edging,** working in ends of rows across long edge, ch 1, sc in top of last st made, ch 5, (sc in top of next row, ch 5) across to row 1, sc in row 1, (ch 5, sc in top of next row) across, fasten off. *(98 ch sps)*
For **second side edging,** working in ends of rows on other side of Strip, join with sc in row 50, (ch 5, sc in top of next row) 25 times

JOINING DIAGRAM

Row 99	Eighth Strip · Row 50
Row 99	Seventh Strip · Row 50
Row 99	Sixth Strip · Row 50
Row 50	Fifth Strip · / Neck / · Ninth Strip · Row 43 — Front Opening
Row 50	Fourth Strip · Tenth Strip · Row 1
Row 99	Third Strip · Row 50
Row 99	Second Strip · Row 50
Row 50	First Strip · Row 99

leaving remaining rows unworked, fasten off.

SECOND STRIP
Rows 1-99: Repeat same rows of First Strip.

For **joined edging,** working in ends of rows across long edge, ch 1, sc in top of last st made; joining to ch sps on long edge of last Strip made (see Joining Diagram), ch 2, sc in first ch sp on other Strip, ch 2, (sc in top of next row on this Strip, ch 2, sc in next ch sp on other Strip, ch 2) across to row 1 on this Strip, sc in row 1, (ch 2, sc in next ch sp on other Strip, ch 2, sc in top of next row on this Strip) across, fasten off.

For **edging,** working in ends of rows on opposite long edge, join with sc in top of row 50, ch 5, (sc in top of next row, ch 5) across to row 1, sc in row 1, (ch 5, sc in top of next row) across. Fasten off.

THIRD STRIP
Rows 1-99: Repeat same rows of First Strip.

For **joined edging,** working in ends of rows across long edge, ch 1, sc in top of last st made; joining to ch sps on long edge of last Strip made, ch 2, sc in first ch sp on other Strip, ch 2, (sc in top of next row on this Strip, ch 2, sc in next ch sp on other Strip, ch 2) across to row 1 on this Strip, sc in row 1, (ch 2, sc in next ch sp on other Strip,

ch 2, sc in top of next row on this Strip) across. Fasten off.

For **first half of edging,** working in ends of rows on opposite long edge of Strip, join with sc in top of row 50, (ch 5, sc in top of next row) 42 times, fasten off; for 2nd half of edging, skip next 9 rows for neck, join with sc in top of next row, (ch 5, sc in next row) across. Fasten off.

FOURTH STRIP
Note: Fourth and Fifth Strips form center back of Jacket below neck.

Rows 1-50: Repeat same rows of First Strip.

For **joined edging,** working in ends of rows across long edge, join with sc in end of row 47; joining to ch sps on long edge of last Strip made, ch 2, sc in first ch sp on other Strip, ch 2, (sc in top of next row on this Strip, ch 2, sc in next ch sp on other Strip, ch 2) across to row 1 on this Strip, sc in row 1 leaving remaining ch sps on other Strip unworked. Fasten off.

For **edging,** working in ends of rows on opposite long edge, join with sc in row 1, (ch 5, sc in top of next row) across, fasten off.

FIFTH STRIP
Rows 1-50: Repeat same rows of First Strip. At end of last row, do **not fasten off.**

For **joined edging,** working in ends of rows across long edge, ch 1, sc in top of last st made; joining to ch sps on long edge

of last Strip made, ch 2, sc in first ch sp on other Strip, ch 2, (sc in top of next row on this Strip, ch 2, sc in next ch sp on other Strip, ch 2) across to row 1 on this Strip, sc in row 1, fasten off.

For **edging,** working in ends of rows on opposite long edge, join with sc in row 1, (ch 5, sc in top of next row) 46 times leaving remaining rows unworked, fasten off.

SIXTH STRIP
Rows 1-99: Repeat same rows of First Strip.

For **joined edging,** working in ends of rows across long edge, ch 1, sc in top of last st made; joining to ch sps on long edge of last Strip made, ch 2, sc in first ch sp on other Strip, ch 2, sc in top of next row on this Strip, (ch 2, sc in next ch sp on other Strip, ch 2, sc in top of next row) 45 times, fasten off; for remainder of edging, skip next 9 rows for neck, join with sc in top of next row, (ch 5, sc in top of next row) across. Fasten off.

For **edging,** working in ends of rows on opposite long edge, join with sc in top of row 50, ch 5, (sc in top of next row, ch 5) across to row 1, sc in row 1, (ch 5, sc in top of next row) across. Fasten off.

SEVENTH STRIP
Work same as Second Strip.

EIGHTH STRIP
Rows 1-99: Repeat same rows of First Strip.

For **joined edging,** working in ends of rows across long edge, ch 1, sc in top of last st made; joining to ch sps on long edge of last Strip made, ch 2, sc in first ch sp on other Strip, ch 2, (sc in top of next row on this Strip, ch 2, sc in next ch sp on other Strip, ch 2) across to row 1 on this Strip, sc in row 1, (ch 2, sc in next ch sp on other Strip, ch 2, sc in top of next row on this Strip) across. Fasten off.

For **edging,** working in ends of

rows on opposite long edge, join with sc in top of row 73, (ch 5, sc in top of next row) across. Fasten off.

NINTH STRIP
Rows 1-43: Repeat same rows of First Strip.

For **joined edging,** working in ends of rows across long edge, ch 1, sc in top of last st made; joining to unworked ch sps on long edge of Sixth Strip, ch 2, sc in first ch sp on other Strip, ch 2, (sc in top of next row on this Strip, ch 2, sc in next ch sp on other Strip, ch 2) across to row 1 on this Strip, sc in row 1. Fasten off.

TENTH STRIP
Rows 1-43: Repeat same rows of First Strip. At end of last row, fasten off.

For **joined edging,** working in ends of rows across long edge, join with sc in row 1; joining to unworked ch sps on long edge of Third Strip, ch 2, sc in last ch sp on other Strip, ch 2, sc in top of next row on this Strip, (ch 2, sc in next ch sp on other Strip, ch 2, sc in top of next row on this Strip) across. Fasten off.

FIRST SIDE SEAM
For **side seam,** fold Eighth Strip in half matching ends of rows, join with sc in top of row 50, ch 2, sc in first ch sp on other end of same Strip, ch 2, sc in top of next row, (ch 2, sc in next ch sp on other Strip, ch 2, sc in top of next row) 24 times leaving remaining rows unworked for armhole. Fasten off.

SECOND SIDE SEAM
For **side seam,** fold First Strip in half matching ends of rows, join with sc in top of row 73 on unworked edge, ch 2, sc in first ch sp on other end of same Strip, ch 2, sc in top of next row, (ch 2, sc in next ch sp on other Strip, ch 2, sc in top of next row) 24 times leaving remaining rows unworked for armhole. Fasten off.

BORDER PINEAPPLES
Pineapple No. 1
Row 1: With right side facing you, working across bottom row of Ninth Strip, join with sl st in first st, ch 3, shell in next shell, ch 3, (dc, ch 3, dc) in next sc, ch 3, skip next ch sp, shell in next shell, dc in last st, turn. *(4 dc, 3 ch sps, 2 shells)*

Row 2: Ch 3, shell in next shell, ch 2, skip next ch sp, 8 tr in next ch sp, ch 2, skip next ch sp, shell in next shell, dc in last st, turn.

Row 3: Ch 3, shell in next shell, ch 2, skip next ch sp, dc in next st, (ch 1, dc in next st) 7 times, ch 2, skip next ch sp, shell in next shell, dc in last st, turn.

Row 4: Ch 3, shell in next shell, ch 3, skip next ch sp, sc in next ch sp, (ch 3, sc in next ch sp) 6 times, ch 3, skip next ch sp, shell in next shell, dc in last st, turn.

Row 5: Ch 3, shell in next shell, ch 3, skip next ch sp, sc in next ch sp, (ch 3, sc in next ch sp) 5 times, ch 3, skip next ch sp, shell in next shell, dc in last st, turn.

Row 6: Ch 3, shell in next shell, ch 3, skip next ch sp, sc in next ch sp, (ch 3, sc in next ch sp) 4 times, ch 3, skip next ch sp, shell in next shell, dc in last st, turn.

Row 7: Ch 3, shell in next shell, ch 3, skip next ch sp, sc in next ch sp, (ch 3, sc in next ch sp) 3 times, ch 3, skip next ch sp, shell in next shell, dc in last st, turn.

Row 8: Ch 3, shell in next shell, ch 3, skip next ch sp, sc in next ch sp, (ch 3, sc in next ch sp) 2 times, ch 3, skip next ch sp, shell in next shell, dc in last st, turn.

Row 9: Ch 3, shell in next shell, ch 3, skip next ch sp, sc in next ch sp, ch 3, sc in next ch sp, ch 3, skip next ch sp, shell in next shell, dc in last st, turn.

Row 10: Ch 3, shell in next shell, ch 3, skip next ch sp, sc in next ch sp, ch 3, skip next ch sp, shell in next shell, dc in last st, turn.

Row 11: Ch 3, shell in next shell, ch 3, skip next 2 ch sps, shell in next shell, dc in last st, turn.

Row 12: Ch 3, shell in next shell, sc in next ch sp, shell in next shell, dc in last st, turn. Fasten off.

For **Pineapple Nos. 2-6,** working across ends of next 5 Strips, work same as First Pineapple.

Pineapple No. 7
Row 1: With right side facing you, working across end of next Strip, join with sl st in first st, ch 3, shell in next shell, ch 3, (dc, ch 3, dc) in next sc, ch 3, skip next ch sp, shell in next shell, dc in last st, turn.

Row 2: Ch 3, shell in next shell, ch 2, skip next ch sp, 8 tr in next ch sp, ch 2, skip next ch sp, shell in next shell, dc in last st, turn.

Row 3: Ch 3, shell in next shell, ch 2, skip next ch sp, dc in next st, (ch 1, dc in next st) 7 times, ch 2, skip next ch sp, shell in next shell, dc in last st, sl st in top of first st on last row of next Strip, turn.

Rows 4-12: Repeat same rows of Pineapple No. 1.

Pineapple Nos. 8-9
Work same as Pineapple No. 1.

Pineapple No. 10
Row 1: With right side facing you, working across end of next Strip, join with sl st in first st, ch 3, shell in next shell, ch 3, (dc, ch 3, dc) in next sc, ch 3, skip next ch sp, shell in next shell, dc in last st, turn.

Row 2: Ch 3, shell in next shell, ch 2, skip next ch sp, 8 tr in next ch sp, ch 2, skip next ch sp, shell in next shell, dc in last st, turn.

Row 3: Ch 3, sl st in top of last st on last row of previous Strip (before Pineapple was added), shell in next shell, ch 2, skip next ch sp, dc in next st, (ch 1, dc in next st) 7 times, ch 2, skip next ch sp, shell in next shell, dc in last st, turn.

Rows 4-12: Repeat same rows of Pineapple No. 1.

For **Pineapple Nos. 11-16,** working across ends of next 6 Strips, work same as Pineapple No. 1.

EDGING
Row 1: Working in ends of rows across right front, join with sl st in top of last row on Strip (before Pineapple was added), 3 sc in

same row, 2 sc in next row, (3 sc in next row, 2 sc in next row) 20 times, skip next row; working in chs, sts and in ends of rows across neck edge, 3 sc in first st, evenly space 150 sc across to last st, 3 sc in last st; working in ends of rows across right front, skip first row, (2 sc in next row, 3 sc in next row) 21 times, sc in top of same row, **do not turn.** Fasten off.

Notes: *For **double crochet cluster (dc cl)**, ch 3, yo, insert hook in third ch from hook, yo, draw lp through, yo, draw through 2 lps on hook, yo, insert hook in same ch, yo, draw lp through, yo, draw through 2 lps on hook, yo, draw through all 3 lps on hook.*

*For **treble crochet cluster (tr cl)**, ch 4, yo 2 times, insert hook in fourth ch from hook, yo, draw lp through, (yo, draw through 2 lps on hook) 2 times, yo 2 times, insert hook in same ch, yo, draw lp through, (yo, draw through 2 lps on hook) 2 times, yo, draw through all 3 lps on hook.*

*For **picot**, ch 3, sl st in top of last st made.*

Rnd 2: Working around outer edge, work this rnd in the following steps;

A: Join with sc in first st of last row, (dc cl, skip next 4 sts, sc in next st) 21 times, tr cl, skip next 7 sts, sc in next st, (tr cl, skip next 6 sts, sc in next st) 20 times, tr cl, skip next 7 sts, sc in next st, dc cl, skip next 5 sts, sc in next st, (dc cl, skip next 4 sts, sc in next st) 20 times;

B: Working across Pineapples, *[picot, ch 3, (dc in top of next row, picot, ch 3) across to end of Pineapple, dc in next shell, picot, ch 3, dc in next sc, picot, ch 3, dc in next shell, picot, ch 3], (dc in top of next row, picot, ch 3) 9 times, dc next row and corresponding row on next Pineapple tog*; repeat between ** 5 more times; ◊repeat between [ ], (dc in top of next row, picot, ch 3) 6 times, dc next row and corresponding row on next Pineapple tog◊; repeat between **; repeat

between ◊◊, repeat between ** 6 times, working across last Pineapple; repeat between [ ], (dc in top of next row, picot, ch 3) across to last row, dc in last row, picot, join with sl st in first sc. Fasten off.

SLEEVES
Pineapple No. 1
Row 1: Working in ends of rows on one armhole, join with sl st in row 5, ch 3, shell in same row, ch 5, skip next 4 rows, (dc, ch 5, dc) in next sc row of row 1, ch 5, skip next 4 rows, (shell, dc) in next row leaving remaining rows unworked, turn. *(4 dc, 3 ch sps, 2 shells made)*

Row 2: Ch 3, shell in next shell, ch 3, skip next ch sp, 11 tr in next ch sp, ch 3, skip next ch sp, shell in next shell, dc in last st, turn.

Row 3: Ch 3, shell in next shell, ch 3, skip next ch sp, dc in next st, (ch 1, dc in next st) 10 times, ch 3, skip next ch sp, shell in next shell, dc in last st, turn.

Row 4: Ch 3, shell in next shell, ch 3, skip next ch sp, sc in next ch sp, (ch 3, sc in next ch sp) 9 times, ch 3, skip next ch sp, shell in next shell, dc in last st, turn.

Row 5: Ch 3, shell in next shell, ch 3, skip next ch sp, sc in next ch sp, (ch 3, sc in next ch sp) 8 times, ch 3, skip next ch sp, shell in next shell, dc in last st, turn.

Row 6: Ch 3, shell in next shell, ch 3, skip next ch sp, sc in next ch sp, (ch 3, sc in next ch sp) 7 times, ch 3, skip next ch sp, shell in next shell, dc in last st, turn.

Row 7: Ch 3, shell in next shell, ch 3, skip next ch sp, sc in next ch sp, (ch 3, sc in next ch sp) 6 times, ch 3, skip next ch sp, shell in next shell, dc in last st, turn.

Row 8: Ch 3, shell in next shell, ch 3, skip next ch sp, sc in next ch sp, (ch 3, sc in next ch sp) 5 times, ch 3, skip next ch sp, shell in next shell, dc in last st, turn.

Row 9: Ch 3, shell in next shell, ch 3, skip next ch sp, sc in next ch sp, (ch 3, sc in next ch sp) 4 times, ch 3, skip next ch sp, shell in next shell, dc in last st, turn.

Row 10: Ch 3, shell in next shell,

ch 3, skip next ch sp, sc in next ch sp, (ch 3, sc in next ch sp) 3 times, ch 3, skip next ch sp, shell in next shell, dc in last st, turn.

Row 11: Ch 3, shell in next shell, ch 3, skip next ch sp, sc in next ch sp, (ch 3, sc in next ch sp) 2 times, ch 3, skip next ch sp, shell in next shell, dc in last st, turn.

Row 12: Ch 3, shell in next shell, ch 3, skip next ch sp, sc in next ch sp, ch 3, sc in next ch sp, ch 3, skip next ch sp, shell in next shell, dc in last st, turn.

Row 13: Ch 3, shell in next shell, ch 3, skip next ch sp, sc in next ch sp, ch 3, skip next ch sp, shell in next shell, dc in last st, turn.

Row 14: Ch 3, shell in next shell, ch 3, skip next 2 ch sps, shell in next shell, dc in last st, turn.

Row 15: Ch 3, shell in next shell, sc in next ch sp, shell in next shell, dc in last st, fasten off.

Pineapple No. 2
Row 1: Skip next 3 rows on armhole, join with sl st in next row, ch 3, shell in same row, ch 3, skip next 3 rows, (dc, ch 5, dc) in next row, ch 3, skip next 3 rows, (shell, dc) in next row leaving remaining rows unworked, turn.

Rows 2-12: Repeat same rows of Border Pineapple No. 1 on page 67.

Pineapple No. 3
Row 1: Skip next 3 rows on armhole, join with sl st in next row, ch 3, shell in same row, ch 5, skip next 3 rows, (tr, ch 5, tr) in next joining sc, ch 5, skip next 3 rows, (shell, dc) in next row leaving remaining rows unworked, turn.

Rows 2-12: Repeat same rows of Border Pineapple No. 1 on page 67.

Pineapple No. 4
Work same as Pineapple No. 2.

Edging
Working in ends of rows and in sts around edges of Pineapples, join with sl st in top of row 4 on Pineapple No. 1, ch 6, sl st in third ch from hook, ch 3, (dc

in top of next row, picot, ch 3) 10 times, dc in next st, picot, ch 3, dc in next shell, picot, ch 3, dc in next sc, picot, ch 3, dc in next shell, picot, ch 3, (dc in top of next row, picot, ch 3) 12 times, dc next row and corresponding row on next Pineapple

tog, picot, ch 3, *(dc in top of next row, picot, ch 3) 8 times, dc in next st, picot, ch 3, dc in next shell, picot, ch 3, dc in next sc, picot, ch 3, dc in next shell, picot, ch 3, (dc in top of next row, picot, ch 3) 8 times, dc next row and corresponding row on

next Pineapple tog, picot, ch 3; repeat from * 2 more times, join with sl st in third ch of ch-6. Fasten off.
Work Sleeve Pineapples and Edging around other armhole.
Weave ribbon through sps between tr cls across neck edging.❑❑

Puff Diamond Table Topper

Designed by Jo Ann Maxwell

FINISHED SIZE:
37" across.

MATERIALS:
❑ 1,900 yds. size 10 crochet cotton thread
❑ No. 5 steel hook or hook size needed to obtain gauge

GAUGE:
Rnds 1-4 = 3¼" across.

BASIC STITCHES:
Ch, sl st, sc, dc, tr.

SPECIAL STITCHES:
For **beginning shell (beg shell)**, ch 3, (dc, ch 2, 2 dc) in same st or sp.

For **shell,** (2 dc, ch 2, 2 dc) in next st or ch sp.

For **picot,** ch 3, sl st in top of last sc made.

For **beginning double shell (beg dbl shell),** ch 3, (dc, ch 2, 2 dc, ch 2, 2 dc) in same sp.

For **double shell (dbl shell),** (2 dc, ch 2, 2 dc, ch 2, 2 dc) in next shell.

For **popcorn (pc),** 5 dc in center ch of specified ch sp, drop lp from hook, insert hook in first st of 5-dc group, draw dropped lp through.

DOILY
Rnd 1: Ch 5, sl st in first ch to form ring, ch 3, 23 dc in ring, join with sl st in top of ch-3. (24 dc made)
Rnd 2: (Ch 3, 2 dc) in first st, ch 3, skip next st, (3 dc in next st, ch 3, skip next st) around, join. (36 dc, 12 ch sps)
Rnd 3: Sl st in next 2 sts, sl st in next ch, ch 3, dc in next 2 chs, ch 3, skip next 3 sts, (dc in next 3 chs, ch 3, skip next 3 sts) around, join.
Rnd 4: Sl st in next st, ch 1, sc in same st, skip next st, 2 dc in next ch, 3 dc in next ch, 2 dc in next ch, (sc in second st of next 3-dc group, skip next st, 2 dc in next ch, 3 dc in next ch, 2 dc in next ch) around, join with sl st in first sc.
Rnd 5: Sl st in next 4 sts, **beg shell** (see Special Stitches), ch 5, skip next 7 sts, (**shell** in next st—see

Special Stitches, ch 5, skip next 7 sts) around, join with sl st in top of ch-3. *(12 shells, 12 ch sps)*

Rnd 6: Sl st in next st, sl st in next ch sp, beg shell, ch 3, sc in next ch sp, picot (see Special Stitches), ch 3, (shell in ch sp of next shell, ch 3, sc in next ch sp, picot, ch 3) around, join.

Rnd 7: Sl st in next st, sl st in next ch sp, beg shell, ch 7, (shell in next shell, ch 7) around, join.

Rnd 8: Sl st in next st, sl st in next ch sp, ch 1, sc in same sp, 2 dc in each of next 3 chs, 3 dc in next ch, 2 dc in each of next 3 chs, (sc in next shell, 2 dc in each of next 3 chs, 3 dc in next ch, 2 dc in each of next 3 chs) around, join with sl st in first sc. *(192 sts)*

Rnd 9: Sl st in next 2 sts, ch 1, sc in same st, *[ch 3, skip next 2 sts, sc in next st, ch 2, skip next 2 sts, shell in next st, ch 2, skip next 2 sts, sc in next st, ch 3, skip next 2 sts, sc in next st, ch 1, skip next 3 sts], sc in next st; repeat from * 10 more times; repeat between [ ], join.

Rnd 10: Sl st in next 3 chs, sl st in next st, sl st in next ch, ch 1, sc in same ch sp, 9 dc in next shell, sc in next ch sp, ch 9, skip next 3 ch sps, (sc in next ch sp, 9 dc in next shell, sc in next ch sp, ch 9, skip next 3 ch sps) around, join.

Rnd 11: Sl st in next 5 sts, beg shell, ch 4, (dc, ch 3, dc) in fifth ch of next ch sp, ch 4, *shell in fifth st of next 9-dc group, ch 4, (dc, ch 3, dc) in fifth ch of next ch sp, ch 4; repeat from * around, join with sl st in top of ch-3.

Rnd 12: Sl st in next st, sl st in next ch sp, beg shell, *[ch 4, sc in next ch sp, 9 dc in next ch sp, sc in next ch sp, ch 4], shell in next shell; repeat from * 10 more times; repeat between [ ], join.

Rnd 13: Sl st in next st, sl st in next ch sp, beg shell, *[ch 3, sc in next ch sp, dc in next dc, (ch 1, dc in next dc) 8 times, sc in next ch sp, ch 3], shell in next shell; repeat from * 10 more times; repeat between [ ], join.

Rnd 14: Sl st in next st, sl st in

next ch sp, **beg dbl shell** *(see Special Stitches)*, *[ch 3, skip next ch sp, sc in next dc, (ch 3, sc in next dc) 8 times, ch 3, skip next ch sp], **dbl shell** *(see Special Stitches)* in next shell; repeat from * 10 more times; repeat between [ ], join.

Rnd 15: Sl st in next st, sl st in next ch sp, beg shell, shell in next ch sp, *[ch 3, skip next ch sp, sc in next ch sp, (ch 3, sc in next ch sp) 7 times, ch 3, skip next ch sp], shell in each of next 2 ch sps of next dbl shell; repeat from * 10 more times; repeat between [ ], join.

Rnd 16: Sl st in next st, sl st in next ch sp, beg shell, *[ch 3, shell in next shell, ch 3, skip next ch sp, sc in next ch sp, (ch 3, sc in next ch sp) 6 times, ch 3, skip next ch sp], shell in next shell; repeat from * 10 more times; repeat between [ ], join.

Rnd 17: Sl st in next st, sl st in next ch sp, beg shell, *[ch 3, **pc** *(see Special Stitches)* in next ch sp, ch 3, shell in next shell, ch 3, skip next ch sp, sc in next ch sp, (ch 3, sc in next ch sp) 5 times, ch 3, skip next ch sp], shell in next shell; repeat from * 10 more times; repeat between [ ], join.

Rnd 18: Sl st in next st, sl st in next ch sp, beg shell, *[ch 3, (pc in next ch sp, ch 3) 2 times, shell in next shell, ch 3, skip next ch sp, sc in next ch sp, (ch 3, sc in next ch sp) 4 times, ch 3, skip next ch sp], shell in next shell; repeat from * 10 more times; repeat between [ ], join.

Rnd 19: Sl st in next st, sl st in next ch sp, beg shell, *[ch 3, (pc in next ch sp, ch 3) 3 times, shell in next shell, ch 3, skip next ch sp, sc in next ch sp, (ch 3, sc in next ch sp) 3 times, ch 3, skip next ch sp], shell in next shell; repeat from * 10 more times; repeat between [ ], join.

Rnd 20: Sl st in next st, sl st in next ch sp, beg dbl shell, *[ch 2, pc in next ch sp, (ch 3, pc in next ch sp) 3 times, ch 2, dbl shell in next shell, ch 3, skip next ch sp, sc in next ch sp, (ch 3,

sc in next ch sp) 2 times, ch 3, skip next ch sp], dbl shell in next shell; repeat from * 10 more times; repeat between [ ], join.

Rnd 21: Sl st in next st, sl st in next ch sp, beg shell, *[ch 3, shell in next ch sp, ch 2, skip next ch sp, pc in next ch sp, (ch 3, pc in next ch sp) 2 times, ch 2, skip next ch sp, shell in next ch sp, ch 3, shell in next ch sp, ch 3, skip next ch sp, sc in next ch sp, ch 3, sc in next ch sp, ch 3, skip next ch sp], shell in next ch sp; repeat from * 10 more times; repeat between [ ], join.

Rnd 22: Sl st in next st, sl st in next ch sp, beg shell, *[ch 3, sc in next ch sp, ch 3, shell in next shell, ch 2, skip next ch sp, pc in next ch sp, ch 3, pc in next ch sp, ch 2, skip next ch sp, shell in next shell, ch 3, sc in next ch sp, ch 3, shell in next shell, ch 3, skip next ch sp, sc in next ch sp, ch 3, skip next ch sp], shell in next shell; repeat from * 10 more times; repeat between [ ], join.

Rnd 23: Sl st in next st, sl st in next ch sp, beg shell, *[ch 4, (sc in next ch sp, ch 4) 2 times, shell in next shell, ch 2, skip next ch sp, pc in next ch sp, ch 2, skip next ch sp, shell in next shell, ch 4, (sc in next ch sp, ch 4) 2 times, shell in next shell, skip 2 ch sps], shell in next shell; repeat from * 10 more times; repeat between [ ], join.

Rnd 24: Sl st in next st, sl st in next ch sp, ch 1, sc in same sp, ch 5, *[(sc in next ch sp, ch 5) 3 times, shell in next shell, skip next pc, shell in next shell, ch 5, (sc in next ch sp, ch 5) 3 times], (sc in next shell, ch 5) 2 times; repeat from * 10 more times; repeat between [ ], sc in last shell; to join, ch 2, dc in first sc *(counts as ch sp)*.

Rnd 25: Beg shell around joining dc, ch 2, sc in next ch sp, (ch 5, sc in next ch sp) 9 times, ch 2, *shell in center of next ch sp, ch 2, sc in next ch sp, (ch 5, sc in next ch sp or in next shell) 9 times, ch 2; repeat from * around, join with sl st in top of ch-3.

Rnd 26: Sl st in next st, sl st in next ch sp, beg dbl shell, *[ch 3, skip next ch sp, sc in next ch sp, (ch 5, sc in next ch sp) 3 times, ch 3, shell in center of next ch sp, ch 3, sc in next ch sp, (ch 5, sc in next ch sp) 3 times, ch 3, skip next ch sp], dbl shell in next shell; repeat from * 10 more times; repeat between [ ], join.

Rnd 27: Sl st in next st, sl st in next ch sp, beg shell, *[ch 3, shell in next ch sp, ch 3, skip next ch sp, sc in next ch sp, (ch 5, sc in next ch sp) 2 times, ch 3, skip next ch sp, dbl shell in next shell, ch 3, skip next ch sp, sc in next ch sp, (ch 5, sc in next ch sp) 2 times, ch 3, skip next ch sp], shell in next ch sp; repeat from * 10 more times; repeat between [ ], join.

Rnd 28: Sl st in next st, sl st in next ch sp, beg shell, *[ch 3, pc in next ch sp, ch 3, shell in next shell, (ch 3, skip next ch sp, sc in next ch sp, ch 5, sc in next ch sp, ch 3, skip next ch sp), shell in next ch sp, ch 3, shell in next ch sp; repeat between ()], shell in next shell; repeat from * 10 more times; repeat between [ ], join.

Rnd 29: Sl st in next st, sl st in next ch sp, beg shell, *[ch 3, (pc in next ch sp, ch 3) 2 times, shell in next shell, ch 3, skip next ch sp, sc in next ch sp, ch 3, skip next ch sp, shell in next shell, ch 3, shell in center of next ch sp, ch 3, shell in next shell, ch 3, skip next ch sp, sc in next ch sp, ch 3, skip next ch sp], shell in next shell; repeat from * 10 more times; repeat between [ ], join.

Rnd 30: Sl st in next st, sl st in next ch sp, beg shell, *[(ch 3, pc in next ch sp) 3 times, ch 3, shell in next shell, ch 4, skip next 2 ch sps, shell in next shell, ch 3, sc in next ch sp, 12 dc in next shell, sc in next ch sp, ch 3, shell in next shell, ch 4, skip next 2 ch sps], shell in next shell; repeat from * 10 more times; repeat between [ ], join.

Rnd 31: Sl st in next st, sl st in next ch sp, beg shell, *[ch 2, pc in next ch sp, (ch 3, pc in next

ch sp) 3 times, ch 2, shell in next shell, ch 4, skip next ch sp, shell in next shell, ch 3, sc in next ch sp, dc in next dc, (ch 1, dc in next dc) 11 times, sc in next ch sp, ch 3, shell in next shell, ch 4, skip next ch sp], shell in next shell; repeat from * 10 more times; repeat between [ ], join.

Rnd 32: Sl st in next st, sl st in next ch sp, beg shell, *[ch 2, skip next ch sp, pc in next ch sp, (ch 3, pc in next ch sp) 2 times, ch 2, skip next ch sp, shell in next shell, ch 4, skip next ch sp, shell in next shell, ch 3, skip next ch sp, sc in next dc, (ch 3, sc in next dc) 11 times, ch 3, skip next ch sp, shell in next shell, ch 4, skip next ch sp], shell in next shell; repeat from * 10 more times; repeat between [ ], join.

Rnd 33: Sl st in next st, sl st in next ch sp, beg shell, *[ch 2, skip next ch sp, pc in next ch sp, ch 3, pc in next ch sp, ch 2, skip next ch sp, shell in next shell, ch 3, sc in next ch sp, ch 3, shell in next shell, ch 3, skip next ch sp, sc in next ch sp, (ch 3, sc in next ch sp) 10 times, ch 3, skip next ch sp, shell in next shell, ch 3, sc in next ch sp, ch 3], shell in next shell; repeat from * 10 more times; repeat between [ ], join.

Rnd 34: Sl st in next st, sl st in next ch sp, beg shell, *[ch 2, skip next ch sp, pc in next ch sp, ch 2, skip next ch sp, shell in next shell, ch 3, (sc in next ch sp, ch 3) 2 times. shell in next shell, ch 3, skip next ch sp, sc in next ch sp, (ch 3, sc in next ch sp) 9 times, ch 3, skip next ch sp, shell in next shell, ch 3, (sc in next ch sp, ch 3) 2 times], shell in next shell; repeat from * 10 more times; repeat between [ ], join.

Rnd 35: Sl st in next st, sl st in next ch sp, beg shell, skip next pc, shell in next shell, *[ch 5, skip next ch sp, sc in next ch sp, ch 5, skip next ch sp, shell in next shell, ch 3, skip next ch sp, sc in next ch sp, (ch 3, sc in next ch sp) 8 times, ch 3, skip next ch sp, shell in next shell, ch 5, skip next ch sp, sc in next ch sp, ch 5, skip

next ch sp], shell in next shell, skip next pc, shell in next shell; repeat from * 10 more times; repeat between [ ], join.

Rnd 36: Sl st in next st, sl st in next ch sp, ch 1, sc in same sp, ch 5, (sc in next shell or in next ch sp, ch 5) 3 times, *[shell in next shell, ch 3, skip next ch sp, sc in next ch sp, (ch 3, sc in next ch sp) 7 times, ch 3, skip next ch sp, shell in next shell], ch 5, (sc in next ch sp or in next shell, ch 5) 6 times; repeat from * 10 more times; repeat between [ ], ch 5, (sc in next ch sp, ch 5) 2 times, join with sl st in first sc.

Rnd 37: Sl st in next 3 chs, beg shell, *[ch 3, (sc in next ch sp, ch 5) 3 times, shell in next shell, ch 3, skip next ch sp, sc in next ch sp, (ch 3, sc in next ch sp) 6 times, ch 3, skip next ch sp, shell in next shell, (ch 5, sc in next ch sp) 3 times, ch 3], shell in next ch sp; repeat from * 10 more times; repeat between [ ], join with sl st in top of ch-3.

Rnd 38: Sl st in next st, sl st in next ch sp, beg dbl shell, *[ch 5, skip next ch sp, (sc in next ch sp, ch 5) 3 times, dbl shell in next shell, ch 3, skip next ch sp, sc in next ch sp, (ch 3, sc in next ch sp) 5 times, ch 3, skip next ch sp, dbl shell in next shell, (ch 5, sc in next ch sp) 3 times, ch 5, skip next ch sp], dbl shell in next shell; repeat from * 10 more times; repeat between [ ], join.

Rnd 39: Sl st in next st, sl st in next ch sp, beg shell, *[ch 3, shell in next ch sp, ch 3, sc in next ch sp, (ch 5, sc in next ch sp) 3 times, ch 3, shell in next ch sp, ch 3, shell in next ch sp, ch 3, skip next ch sp, sc in next ch sp, (ch 3, sc in next ch sp) 4 times, ch 3, skip next ch sp, shell in next ch sp, ch 3, shell in next ch sp, ch 3, sc in next ch sp, (ch 5, sc in next ch sp) 3 times, ch 3], shell in next ch sp; repeat from * 10 more times; repeat between [ ], join.

Rnd 40: Sl st in next st, sl st in next ch sp, beg shell, ◊[*ch 4, sc in next ch sp, ch 4, shell in next shell, ch 3, skip next ch sp, sc in next ch sp, (ch 5, sc in next ch sp) 2 times, ch 3, skip next ch sp*, shell in next shell, ch 4, sc in next ch sp, ch 4, shell in next shell, ch 3, skip next ch sp, sc in next ch sp, (ch 3, sc in next ch sp) 3 times, ch 3, skip next ch sp, shell in next shell; repeat between **◊, shell in next shell]; repeat between [ ] 10 more times; repeat between ◊◊, join.

Rnd 41: Sl st in next st, sl st in next ch sp, beg shell, ◊[*ch 3, sc in next ch sp, ch 5, sc in next ch sp, ch 3, shell in next shell, ch 3, skip next ch sp, sc in next ch sp, ch 5, sc in next ch sp, ch 3, skip next ch sp*, shell in next shell, ch 3, sc in next ch sp, ch 5, sc in next ch sp, ch 3, shell in next shell, ch 3, skip next ch sp, sc in next ch sp, (ch 3, sc in next ch sp) 2 times, ch 3, skip next ch sp, shell in next shell; repeat between **◊, shell in next shell]; repeat between [ ] 10 more times; repeat between ◊, join.

Rnd 42: Sl st in next st, sl st in next ch sp, beg shell, ◊[*ch 3, sc in next ch sp, (ch 5, sc in next ch sp) 2 times, ch 3, shell in next shell, ch 3, skip next ch sp, sc in next ch sp, ch 3, skip next ch sp*, shell in next shell, ch 3, sc in next ch sp, (ch 5, sc in next ch sp) 2 times, ch 3, shell in next shell, ch 3, skip next ch sp, sc in next ch sp, ch 3, sc in next ch sp, ch 3, skip next ch sp, shell

in next shell; repeat between **◊, shell in next shell]; repeat between [ ] 10 more times; repeat between ◊◊, join.

Rnd 43: Sl st in next st, sl st in next ch sp, beg shell, ◊[*ch 3, sc in next ch sp, (ch 5, sc in next ch sp) 3 times, ch 3*, shell in next shell, skip next 2 ch sps, shell in next shell; repeat between **, shell in next shell, ch 3, skip next ch sp, sc in next ch sp, ch 3, skip next ch sp, shell in next shell; repeat between **, shell in next shell, skip next 2 ch sps◊, shell in next shell]; repeat between [ ] 10 more times; repeat between ◊◊, join.

Rnd 44: Sl st in next st, sl st in next ch sp, ch 1, sc in same sp, *[(ch 5, sc in next ch sp) 5 times, ch 5, sc in next shell, ch 1, sc in next shell, (ch 5, sc in next ch sp) 5 times, ch 3, shell in next shell, skip next 2 ch sps, shell in next shell, ch 3, sc in next ch sp, (ch 5, sc in next ch sp) 4 times, ch 5, sc in next shell, ch 1], sc in next shell; repeat from * 10 more times; repeat between [ ], join with sl st in first sc.

Rnd 45: Sl st in next 3 chs, ch 1, sc in same sp, (ch 5, sc in next ch-5 sp or in next shell) around skipping ch-1 sps and ch-3 sps on each side of shells; to join, ch 2, dc in first sc (counts as ch sp). (216 ch sps)

Rnd 46: Beg pc around joining dc, ch 4, sc in next ch sp, picot, ch 4, (pc in next ch sp, ch 4, sc in next ch sp, picot, ch 4) around, join with sl st in top of beg pc.

Rnd 47: Ch 1, sc in first pc, ch 9, (sc in next pc, ch 9) around, join with sl st in first sc.

Rnd 48: Sl st in next ch, ch 3, (2 dc in next ch, dc in next ch) 4 times, sc in next ch lp, ch 1, shell in fifth ch of same lp, ch 1, sc in same lp, *dc in first ch of next ch lp, (2 dc in next ch, dc in next ch) 4 times, sc in next ch lp, ch 1, shell in fifth ch of same lp, ch 1, sc in same lp; repeat from * around, join with sl st in top of ch-3.

Rnd 49: Sl st in next st, ch 6 (counts as first tr and ch-2 sp), tr in next st, (ch 2, tr in next st) 9 times, sc in next shell, *tr in second st of next 13-dc group, (ch 2, tr in next st) 10 times, sc in next shell; repeat from * around, join with sl st in fourth ch of ch-6.

Note: For **picot** on next rnd, ch 4, sl st in top of last st made.

Rnd 50: Ch 1, sc in first st, *[(5 dc in next tr, sc in next tr) 2 times, (4 dc, picot, 3 dc) in next tr, sc in next tr, (5 dc in next tr, sc in next tr) 2 times, skip next sc], sc in next tr; repeat from * around to last 10 tr; repeat between [ ], join with sl st in first sc. Fasten off.❑❑

Pineapple Poncho

Designed by Margret Willson

FINISHED SIZE:
One size fits all. Measures 36½" from neckline to center bottom point.

MATERIALS:
- ❑ 28 oz. peach worsted yarn
- ❑ Tapestry needle
- ❑ H crochet hook or hook size needed to obtain gauge

GAUGE:
7 dc = 2"; 7 dc rows = 4". Pineapple Block is 10½" square. Rectangle is 11" x 19¾".

BASIC STITCHES:
Ch, sl st, sc, dc, tr.

SPECIAL STITCHES:
For **beginning shell (beg shell)**, ch 3, (dc, ch 2, 2 dc) in same ch sp.

For **shell**, (2 dc, ch 2, 2 dc) in next ch sp.

For **puff stitch (puff st)**, yo, insert hook in next st, yo, draw up long lp, (yo, insert hook in same st, yo, draw up long lp) 2 times, yo, draw through all 7 lps on hook.

For **2-treble cluster (2-tr cl)**, yo 2 times, insert hook in next st, yo, draw lp through, (yo, draw through 2 lps on hook) 2 times, yo 2 times, insert hook in same st, yo, draw lp through, (yo, draw through 2 lps on hook) 2 times, yo, draw through all 3 lps on hook.

For **3-treble cluster (3-tr cl)**, yo 2 times, insert hook in next st, yo, draw lp through, (yo, draw through 2 lps on hook) 2 times, *yo 2 times, insert hook in same st, yo, draw lp through, (yo, draw through 2 lps on hook) 2 times; repeat from *, yo, draw through all 4 lps on hook.

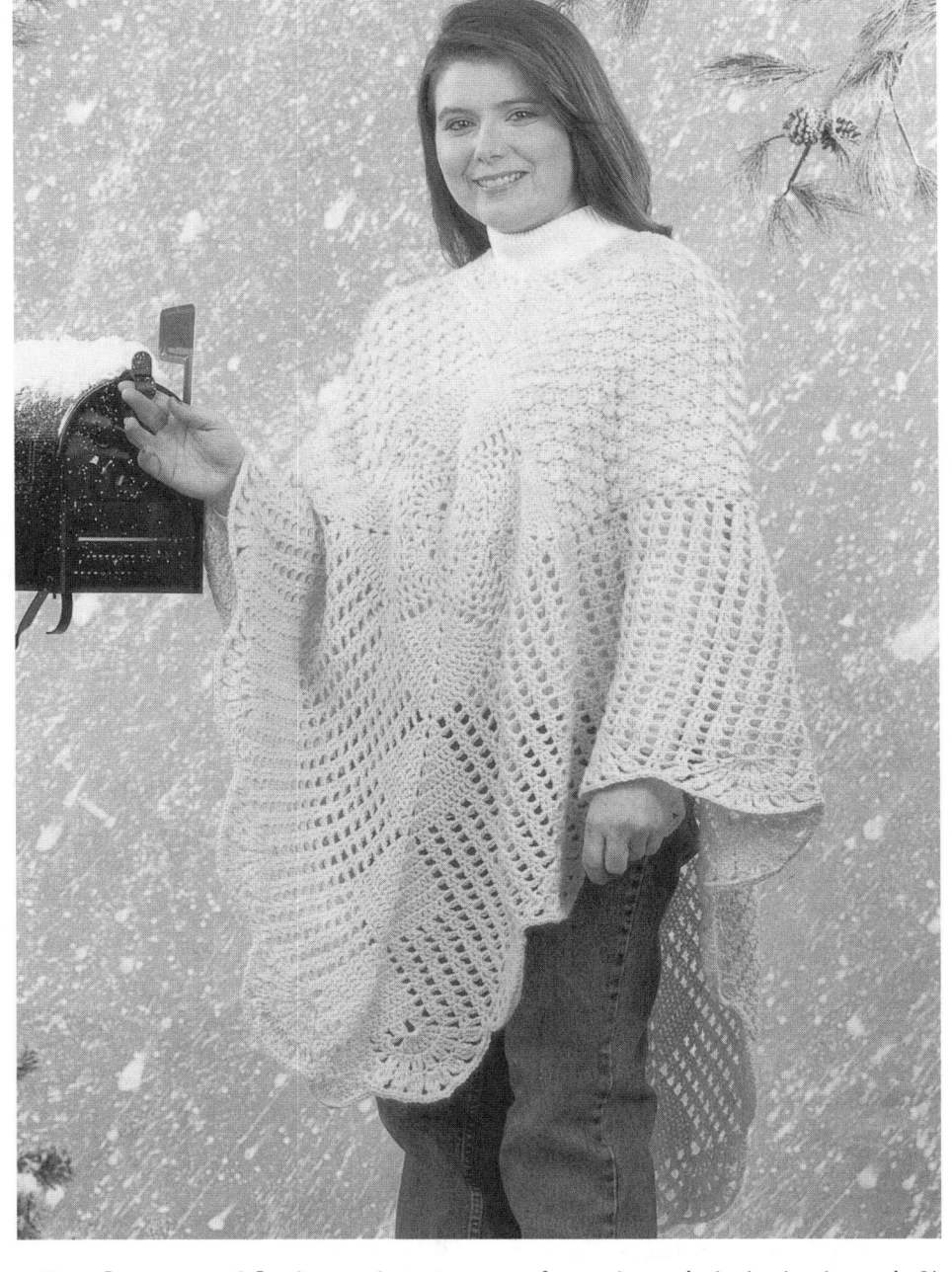

For **decrease (dec)**, yo, insert hook in next st, yo, draw lp through, yo, draw through 2 lps on hook, skip next 3 sts, yo, insert hook in next st, yo, draw lp through, yo, draw through 2 lps on hook, yo, draw through all 3 lps on hook.

PINEAPPLE BLOCK (make 2)
Rnd 1: Ch 4, sl st in first ch to form ring, ch 1, (sc in ring, ch 3) 4 times, join with sl st in first sc. *(4 sc, 4 ch-3 sps made)*

Rnd 2: Sl st in next ch sp, **beg shell** *(see Special Stitches)*, dc in next st, ***shell** *(see Special Stitches)* in next ch sp, dc in next st; repeat from * around, join with sl st in top of ch-3. *(4 shells, 4 dc)*

Rnd 3: Sl st in next st, sl st in next ch sp, beg shell, *[skip next 2 sts, (dc, ch 3, dc) in next st], shell in next ch sp; repeat from * 2 more times; repeat between [ ], join.

Rnd 4: Sl st in next st, sl st in next ch sp, beg shell, 7 dc in next ch sp, (shell in next ch sp, 7 dc in next ch sp) around, join.

Rnd 5: Sl st in next st, sl st in next ch sp, beg shell, *[skip next 2 sts, dc in next st, (ch 1, dc in next st) 6 times], shell in next ch sp; repeat from * 2 more times; repeat between [ ], join.

Rnd 6: Sl st in next st, sl st in next ch sp, beg shell, *[ch 2, sc in next ch sp, (ch 3, sc in next ch sp) 5 times, ch 2], shell in next ch sp; repeat from * 2 more times; repeat between [ ], join.

Rnd 7: Ch 3, dc in next st, *[shell in next ch sp, dc in next 2 sts, ch 2, skip next ch sp, sc in next ch sp, (ch 3, sc in next ch sp) 4 times, ch 2], dc in next 2 sts; repeat from * 2 more times; repeat between [ ], join.

Rnd 8: Ch 3, dc in next 3 sts, *[shell in next ch sp, dc in next 4 sts, ch 2, skip next ch sp, sc in next ch sp, (ch 3, sc in next ch sp) 3 times, ch 2], dc in next 4 sts; repeat from * 2 more times; repeat between [ ], join.

Rnd 9: Ch 3, dc in next 5 sts, *[shell in next ch sp, dc in next 6 sts, ch 2, skip next ch sp, sc in next ch sp, (ch 3, sc in next ch sp) 2 times, ch 2], dc in next 6 sts; repeat from * 2 more times; repeat between [ ], join.

Rnd 10: Ch 3, dc in next 7 sts, *[shell in next ch sp, dc in next 8 sts, ch 2, skip next ch sp, sc in next ch sp, ch 3, sc in next ch sp, ch 2], dc in next 8 sts; repeat from * 2 more times; repeat between [ ], join.

Rnd 11: Ch 3, dc in next 9 sts, *[shell in next ch sp, dc in next 10 sts, ch 2, skip next ch sp, sc in next ch sp, ch 2], dc in next 10 sts; repeat from * 2 more times; repeat between [ ], join.

Rnd 12: Ch 3, dc in next 11 sts, *[shell in next ch sp, dc in next 12 sts, skip next ch sp, 4 dc in next st, skip next ch sp], dc in

next 12 sts; repeat from * 2 more times; repeat between [ ], join. Fasten off.

RECTANGLE (make 2)
Row 1: Ch 40, dc in fourth ch from hook, dc in each ch across, turn. *(38 dc made)*

Row 2: Ch 1, sc in first st, **puff st** *(see Special Stitches)* in next st, (sc in next 2 sts, puff st in next st) across to last 3 sts, sc in last 3 sts, turn. *(26 sc, 12 puff sts)*

Row 3: Ch 3, dc in each st across, turn. *(38 dc)*

Row 4: Ch 1, sc in first 2 sts, (puff st in next st, sc in next 2 sts) across, turn.

Row 5: Ch 3, dc in each st across, turn.

Rows 6-45: Repeat rows 2-5 consecutively. At end of last row, fasten off.

Holding Pineapple Blocks and Rectangles wrong sides together, easing to fit, matching lettered edges, sew short edges together through **back lps** *(see Stitch Guide)* according to assembly illustration.

Assembly Illustration

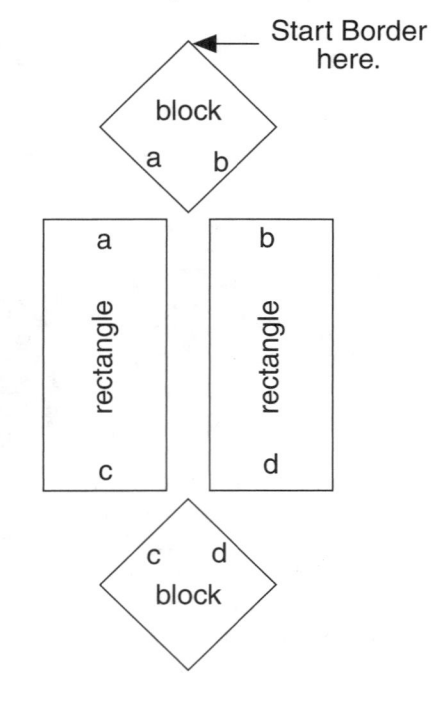

Start Border here.

block
a   b

a   b

rectangle   rectangle

c   d

c   d
block

BORDER
Rnd 1: Working around outer edge of Pineapple Blocks and

Rectangles, join with sl st in corner ch sp on one Pineapple Block *(see assembly illustration),* beg shell, *ch 2, skip next 2 sts, dc in next 2 sts, (ch 2, skip next st, dc in next 2 sts) 4 times, ch 2, (dc in next 2 sts, ch 2, skip next st) 5 times, dc in next st, dc in next ch sp, ch 2; working in ends of rows across next Rectangle, 2 dc in first dc row, (ch 2, skip next sc row, 2 dc in next dc row) 22 times, ch 2, dc in next ch sp on next Pineapple Block, dc in next st, (ch 2, skip next st, dc in next 2 sts) 5 times, ch 2, dc in next 2 sts, (ch 2, skip next st, dc in next 2 sts) 4 times, ch 2, skip next 2 sts* shell in next corner ch sp; repeat between **, join with sl st in top of ch-3. *(90 2-dc groups, 2 shells)*

Rnd 2: Ch 3, dc in next st, *shell in next ch sp, dc in next 2 sts, ch 2, skip next ch sp, (dc in next 2 sts, ch 2, skip next ch sp) across* to 2 sts before next corner ch sp, dc in next 2 sts; repeat between **, join.

Rnd 3: Ch 3, dc in next 3 sts, *shell in next ch sp, dc in next 4 sts, ch 2, skip next ch sp, (dc in next 2 sts, ch 2, skip next ch sp) across* to 4 sts before next corner ch sp, dc in next 4 sts; repeat between **, join.

Rnd 4: Ch 3, dc in next 5 sts, *shell in next ch sp, dc in next 6 sts, ch 2, skip next ch sp, (dc in next 2 sts, ch 2, skip next ch sp) across* to 6 sts before next corner ch sp, dc in next 6 sts; repeat between **, join.

Rnd 5: Ch 3, dc in next 7 sts, *shell in next ch sp, dc in next 8 sts, ch 2, skip next ch sp, (dc in next 2 sts, ch 2, skip next ch sp) across* to 8 sts before next corner ch sp, dc in next 8 sts; repeat between **, join.

Rnd 6: Ch 3, dc in next 9 sts, *shell in next ch sp, dc in next 10 sts, ch 2, skip next ch sp, (dc in next 2 sts, ch 2, skip next ch sp) across* to 10 sts before next corner ch sp, dc in next 10 sts; repeat between **, join.

Rnd 7: Ch 3, dc in next st, ch 2,

skip next st, (dc in next 2 sts, ch 2, skip next st) 3 times, *shell in next ch sp, ch 2, skip next st or ch sp, (dc in next 2 sts, ch 2, skip next st or ch sp) across* to next corner ch sp*; repeat between **, join.

Rnd 8: Ch 3, dc in next st, *(ch 2, skip next ch sp, dc in next 2 sts) across] to next corner ch sp, shell in next ch sp, dc in next 2 sts; repeat from *; repeat between [ ], ch 2, join.

Rnd 9: Ch 3, dc in next st, *[ch 2, skip next ch sp, (dc in next 2 sts, ch 2, skip next ch sp) across] to 4 sts before next corner ch sp, dc in next 4 sts, shell in next ch sp, dc in next 4 sts; repeat from *; repeat between [ ], join.

Rnd 10: Ch 3, dc in next st, *[ch 2, skip next ch sp, (dc in next 2 sts, ch 2, skip next ch sp) across] to 6 sts before next corner ch sp, dc in next 6 sts, shell in next ch sp, dc in next 6 sts; repeat from *; repeat between [ ], join.

Rnd 11: Ch 3, dc in next st, *[ch 2, skip next ch sp, (dc in next 2 sts, ch 2, skip next ch sp) across] to 8 sts before next corner ch sp, dc in next 8 sts, shell in next ch sp, dc in next 8 sts; repeat from *; repeat between [ ], join.

Rnd 12: Ch 3, dc in next st, *[ch 2, skip next ch sp, (dc in next 2 sts, ch 2, skip next ch sp) across] to 10 sts before next corner ch sp, dc in next 10 sts, shell in next ch sp, dc in next 10 sts; repeat from *; repeat between [ ], join.

Rnd 13: Ch 3, dc in next st, *[ch 2, skip next ch sp or st, (dc in next 2 sts, ch 2, skip next ch sp or st) across] to next corner ch sp, shell in next ch sp; repeat from *; repeat between [ ], join.

Rnds 14-19: Repeat rnds 8-13, ending with 69 2-dc groups between each corner ch sp on last rnd.

Rnd 20: Ch 3, dc in next st, skip next ch sp, 7 tr in next ch sp, skip next ch sp, dc in next 2 sts, (ch 2, skip next ch sp, dc in next 2 sts) 4 times, skip next ch sp, [7 tr in next ch sp, skip next ch sp, dc in next 2 sts, (ch 2, skip next ch sp, dc in next 2 sts) 2 times], shell in next ch sp, dc in next 2 sts, (ch 2, skip next ch sp, dc in next 2 sts) 2 times, skip next ch sp, *7 tr in next ch sp, skip next ch sp, dc in next 2 sts, (ch 2, skip next ch sp, dc in next 2 sts) 4 times, skip next ch sp*; repeat between ** 8 more times; repeat between [ ]; repeat between ** 7 more times, 7 tr in next ch sp, skip next ch sp, (dc in next 2 sts, ch 2, skip next ch sp) 4 times, join. Fasten off.

Rnd 21: Join with sl st in any corner ch sp, beg shell, ◊ch 2, skip next 2 sts, dc in next 2 sts, ch 2, skip next ch sp, dc in next 2 sts, *[skip next 2 dc, 2-tr cl (see Special Stitches) in next tr, (ch 1, 2-tr cl in next tr) 6 times, skip next 2 dc, dc in next 2 sts], (ch 2, skip next ch sp, dc in next 2 sts) 2 times; repeat from * 8 more times; repeat between [ ], ch 2, skip next ch sp, dc in next 2 sts, ch 2, skip next 2 sts◊, shell in next corner ch sp; repeat between ◊◊, join.

Rnd 22: Ch 3, dc in next dc, [shell in next ch sp, dc in next 2 dc, ch 2, skip next ch sp, dc in next 2 dc, *3-tr cl (see Special Stitches) in next cl, (ch 3, 3-tr cl in next cl) 2 times, ch 3, (3-tr cl, ch 3, 3-tr cl) in next cl, (ch 3, 3-tr cl in next cl) 3 times, skip next 2 dc and ch sp, dc in next 2 dc; repeat from * 9 more times; ch 2], dc in next 2 dc; repeat between [ ], join.

Rnd 23: Ch 1, sc in each st and 3 sc in each ch sp around, join with sl st in first sc. Fasten off.

YOKE

Rnd 1: Working around neckline in ends of rows, join with sl st in first row of one Rectangle, ch 3, dc in same row, *dc in next sc row, (2 dc in next dc row, dc in next sc row) 3 times, ch 2, 2 dc in next dc row, (ch 2, skip next sc, row, 2 dc in next dc row) 14 times, ch 2, (dc in next sc row, 2 dc in next dc row) 4 times*, 2 dc in next dc row on next rectangle; repeat between **, join with sl st in top of ch-3. (48 dc, 30 2-dc groups made)

Rnd 2: Sl st in next 2 sts, ch 3, dc in next 9 sts, *ch 2, (dc in next 2 sts, ch 2, skip next ch sp) 15 times*, dc in next 9 sts, dec (see Special Stitches), dc in next 9 sts; repeat between **, dc in next 10 sts, skip last 3 sts, join. (38 dc, 30 2 dc groups)

Rnd 3: Sl st in next 2 sts, ch 3, dc in next 7 sts, *ch 2, (dc in next 2 sts, ch 2, skip next ch sp) 15 times*, dc in next 7 sts, dec, dc in next 7 sts; repeat between **, dc in next 8 sts, skip remaining sts, join.

Rnd 4: Sl st in next 2 sts, ch 3, dc in next 5 sts, *ch 2, (dc in next 2 sts, ch 2, skip next ch sp) 15 times*, dc in next 5 sts, dec, dc in next 5 sts; repeat between **, dc in next 6 sts, skip remaining sts, join.

Rnd 5: Sl st in next 2 sts, ch 3, dc in next 3 sts, *ch 2, (dc in next 2 sts, ch 2, skip next ch sp) 15 times*, dc in next 3 sts, dec, dc in next 3 sts; repeat between **, dc in next 4 sts, skip remaining sts, join.

Rnd 6: Sl st in next 2 sts, ch 2, dc in next st, *ch 2, (dc in next 2 sts, ch 2, skip next ch sp) 15 times*, dc in next st, dec, dc in next st; repeat between **, dc in next 2 sts, skip remaining sts, join. Fasten off.❑❑

Cluster Pineapple Doily

Designed by Navonda Maxwell

FINISHED SIZE:
25" across.

MATERIALS:
- ❑ 700 yds. lavender size 10 crochet cotton thread
- ❑ No. 5 steel hook or hook size needed to obtain gauge

GAUGE:
Rnds 1-4 = 2¾" across.

BASIC STITCHES:
Ch, sl st, sc, dc.

SPECIAL STITCHES:
For **beginning shell (beg shell),** (sl st, ch 3, dc, ch 2, 2 dc) in first ch sp.

For **shell,** (2 dc, ch 2, 2 dc) in st or ch sp specified in instructions.

For **cluster, yo,** insert hook in st specified in instructions, yo, pull through, yo, pull through 2 lps on hook, (yo, insert hook in same st, yo, pull through, yo, pull through 2 lps on hook) 4 times, yo, pull through all lps on hook.

For **picot,** ch 3, sl st in top of last st made.

DOILY
Rnd 1: Ch 8, sl st in first ch to form ring, ch 3, 27 dc in ring, join with sl st in top of ch-3. *(28 dc made)*

Rnds 2-3: (Ch 3, dc) in first st, dc in next st, (2 dc in next st, dc in next st) around, join. *(42, 63)*

Rnd 4: Ch 3, dc in each st around with 2 dc in last st, join. *(64)*

Rnd 5: Ch 1, sc in first st, ch 3, skip next st, (sc in next st, ch 3, skip next st) around, join with sl st in first sc. *(32 ch sps)*

Rnd 6: Sl st across to center ch of first ch sp, ch 1, sc in same ch sp, ch 4, (sc in next ch sp, ch 4) around, join.

Rnd 7: Sl st across to second ch of first ch sp, ch 1, sc in same ch sp, ch 5, (sc in next ch sp, ch 5) around, join.

Rnds 8-9: Sl st across to third ch of first ch sp, ch 1, sc in same ch sp, ch 6, (sc in next ch sp, ch 6) around, join.

Rnds 10-12: Sl st across to third ch of first ch sp, ch 1, sc in same ch sp, ch 7, (sc in next ch sp, ch 7) around, join.

Rnd 13: Sl st across to center ch of first ch sp, (sl st, ch 3, dc, ch 2, 2 dc) in center ch, *(beg shell made)*, ch 4, *(2 dc, ch 2, 2 dc) in center ch of next ch sp *(shell made)*, ch 4; repeat from * around, join with sl st in top of ch-3.

Rnd 14: Sl st in next st, beg shell in ch sp of first **shell** *(see Special Stitches)*, ch 6, skip next ch sp, *shell in ch sp of next **shell** *(see Special Stitches)*, ch 6, skip next ch sp; repeat from * around, join.

Rnd 15: Sl st in next st, beg shell, ch 7, skip next ch sp, (shell in next shell, ch 7, skip next ch sp) around, join.

Rnd 16: Sl st in next st, beg shell, ch 3, sc in next ch sp two rnds below, ch 3, (shell in next shell, ch 3, sc in next ch sp two rnds below, ch 3) around, join.

Rnd 17: Sl st in next st, beg shell,

ch 7, skip next 2 ch sps, (shell in next shell, ch 7, skip next 2 ch sps) around, join.

Rnd 18: Sl st in next st, beg shell, ch 3, sc in next ch sp, ch 3, (shell in next shell, ch 3, sc in next ch sp, ch 3) around, join.

Rnd 19: Sl st in next st, beg shell, ch 8, skip next 2 ch sps, (shell in next shell, ch 8, skip next 2 ch sps) around, join.

Rnd 20: Sl st in next st, beg shell, ch 4, sc in next ch sp, ch 4, (shell in next shell, ch 4, sc in next ch sp, ch 4) around, join.

Rnd 21: Sl st in next st, beg shell, *[ch 7, skip next 2 ch sps, 2 dc in first st of next shell, dc in next st, 4 dc in next ch sp, dc in next st, 2 dc in next st, ch 7, skip next 2 ch sps], shell in next shell; repeat from * 14 more times; repeat between [-], join.

Rnd 22: Sl st in next st, beg shell, *[ch 8, skip next ch sp, 2 dc in next st, dc in next 8 sts, 2 dc in next st, ch 8, skip next ch sp], shell in next shell; repeat from * 14 more times; repeat between [-], join.

Rnd 23: Sl st in next st, beg shell shell, *[ch 5, sc in next ch sp two rnds below, ch 1, dc in next st, (ch 1, dc in next st) 11 times, ch 1, sc in next ch sp two rnds below, ch 5], shell in next shell; repeat from * 14 more times; repeat between [-], join.

Rnd 24: Sl st in next st, beg shell, *[ch 7, skip next 2 ch sps, sc in next ch sp, (ch 3, sc in next ch sp) 10 times, ch 7, skip next 2 ch sps], shell in next shell; repeat from * 14 more times; repeat between [-], join.

Rnd 25: Sl st in next st, beg shell, *[ch 8, skip next ch sp, sc in next ch sp, (ch 3, sc in next ch sp) 9 times, ch 8, skip next ch sp], shell in next shell; repeat from * 14 more times; repeat between [-], join.

Rnd 26: Sl st in next st, (beg shell, ch 2, 2 dc) in first shell, *[ch 8, skip next ch sp, sc in next ch sp, (ch 3, sc in next ch sp) 8 times, ch 8, skip next ch sp], (shell, ch 2, 2 dc) in next shell; repeat from * 14 more times; repeat between [-], join.

Rnd 27: Sl st in next st, beg shell, *[ch 1, shell in next ch sp, ch 8, skip next ch sp, sc in next ch sp, (ch 3, sc in next ch sp) 7 times, ch 8, skip next ch sp], shell in next shell; repeat from * 14 more times; repeat between [-], join.

Rnd 28: Sl st in next st, beg shell, *[ch 3, sc in next ch sp, ch 3, shell in next shell, ch 8, skip next ch sp, sc in next ch sp, (ch 3, sc in next ch sp) 6 times, ch 8, skip next ch sp], shell in next shell; repeat from * 14 more times; repeat between [-], join.

Rnd 29: Sl st in next st, beg shell, *◊(ch 3, sc in next ch sp) 2 times, ch 3, shell in next shell, ch 8, skip next ch sp, sc in next ch sp, (ch 3, sc in next ch sp) 5 times, ch 8, skip next ch sp◊, shell in next shell; repeat from * 14 more times; repeat between ◊◊, join.

Rnd 30: Sl st in next st, beg shell, *[ch 7, skip next ch sp, **cluster** in center ch of next ch sp (see *Special Stitches*), ch 7, skip next ch sp, shell in next shell, ch 8, skip next ch sp, sc in next ch sp, (ch 3, sc in next ch sp) 4 times, ch 8, skip next ch sp], shell in next shell; repeat from * 14 more times; repeat between [-], join.

Rnd 31: Sl st in next st, beg shell, *◊(ch 7, cluster in center ch of next ch sp) 2 times, ch 7, shell in next shell, ch 8, skip next ch sp, sc in next ch sp, (ch 3, sc in next ch sp) 3 times, ch 8, skip next ch sp◊, shell in next shell; repeat from * 14 more times; repeat between ◊◊, join.

Rnd 32: Sl st in next st, beg shell, *◊(ch 7, cluster in center ch of next ch sp) 3 times, ch 7, shell in next shell, ch 8, skip next ch sp, sc in next ch sp, (ch 3, sc in next ch sp) 2 times, ch 8, skip next ch sp◊, shell in next shell; repeat from * 14 more times; repeat between ◊◊, join.

Rnd 33: Sl st in next st, beg shell, *[ch 7, sc in next ch sp, (ch 7, cluster in center ch of next ch sp) 2 times, ch 7, sc in next ch sp, ch 7, shell in next shell, ch 8, skip next ch sp, sc in next ch sp, ch 3, sc in next ch sp, ch 8, skip next ch sp], shell in next shell; repeat from * 14 more times; repeat between [-], join.

Rnd 34: Sl st in next st, beg shell, *◊(ch 8, sc in next ch sp) 2 times, ch 8, cluster in center ch of next ch sp, (ch 8, sc in next ch sp) 2 times, ch 8, shell in next shell, ch 8, skip next ch sp, sc in next ch sp, ch 8, skip next ch sp◊, shell in next shell; repeat from * 14 more times; repeat between ◊◊, join.

Rnd 35: Sl st in next st, beg shell, *◊(ch 9, sc in next ch sp) 3 times, ch 11, (sc in next ch sp, ch 9) 3 times◊, shell in each of next 2 shells; repeat from * 14 more times, repeat between ◊◊, shell in last shell, join.

Rnd 36: Sl st in next st, ch 1, sc in first ch sp, *[ch 5, sc in next ch sp, **picot** (see Special Stitches), ch 2, (dc in next ch, 2 dc in next ch) 4 times, dc in next ch, ch 2, sc in next ch sp, picot, ch 2, (dc in next ch, 2 dc in next ch) 5 times, dc in next ch, ch 2, sc in next ch sp, picot, ch 2, (dc in next ch, 2 dc in next ch) 4 times, dc in next ch, ch 2, sc in next ch sp, picot, ch 5], sc in ch sp of next 2 shells; repeat from * 14 more times; repeat between [-], sc in ch sp of last shell, join with sl st in first sc. Fasten off.◻◻

How to Select a Pineapple

The color of a pineapple's shell does not always indicate how sweet or ripe the inside might be. A green colored shell might be as ripe as a golden colored shell. Look for a pineapple that has a fresh appearance with deep green leaves when selecting a pineapple at the grocery store. Try avoiding fruits that have bruises or soft spots. After getting your pineapple home, remember to refrigerate it to preserve its freshness.

History of Pineapples

In 1493, Christopher Columbus brought pineapples back to Queen Isabella of Spain after he found them growing on the island of Guadeloupe. After that, pineapples became very popular and were grown in greenhouses throughout Europe.

Pineapple Fruit Shake
Yield: 2 servings

1 Medium banana
½ c Quartered strawberries
½ c Pineapple or mango cut into chunks
¾ c Orange juice
1 c Ice

Put all ingredients into blender; puree until very smooth and thick.

How Pineapple Got Its Name

The scientific name for pineapple is Ananas cosmosus. It is a tropical fruit native to Central and South America. Spanish explorers thought that a pineapple looked like a pinecone, so they called it "Pina." The English added "apple" to relate it with juicy delicious fruits.

Pineapple Upside Down Cake

¾ cup butter
20 ounces pineapple rings in juice — sliced in half
1 teaspoon baking powder
5 eggs — separated
8 tablespoons pineapple juice

1½ cups brown sugar
1 cup walnuts — chopped coarse
1½ cups flour
¼ teaspoon salt
1½ cups sugar

Preheat oven to 375 degrees. Use 13x9 pan. Melt butter and brown sugar in pan. Arrange pineapple slices in any pattern in pan and cover with walnuts. Set aside. Beat yolks, add sugar and juice. Add flour, baking powder and salt. Fold in beaten egg whites and pour on top of pineapple mixture in pan. Bake for 40-45 minutes. Cool 5 minutes and invert on serving plate. Cool completely.